CW01023931

No Traveller Returns

VAHNI CAPILDEO was born in 1973, in Port-of-Spain, Trinidad. She came to England in 1991. This is her first book.

No Traveller Returns

Vahni Capildeo

SALT

PUBLISHED BY SALT PUBLISHING
PO Box 937, Great Wilbraham PDO, Cambridge CB1 5JX United Kingdom
PO Box 202, Applecross, Western Australia 6153

© Vahni Capildeo, 2003

The right of Vahni Capildeo to be identified as the
author of this work has been asserted by her in accordance
with Section 77 of the Copyright, Designs and Patents Act 1988.

First published 2003

Printed and bound in the United Kingdom by Lightning Source

Typeset in Swift 9.5 / 13

ISBN 1 876857 88 9 paperback

SP

1 3 5 7 9 8 6 4 2

For my parents
Devendranath Capildeo and Leila Bissoondath Capildeo

Contents

Acknowledgments

Thanks are due to the editors of the following magazines: *First Time, Poetry Wales, Southfields, Weyfarers.*

I should like to thank: Brian Catling; Catherine Chin; Sarah Colvin; Peter Conrad; Emma Dillon; David Groiser; Siân Gronlie; Ira Mathur; Rod Mengham; Bernard O'Donoghue; Heather O'Donoghue; Sarah Simblet; Marilyn Strathern.

VAHNI CAPILDEO
January 2003

The Mask in the Bone

Amulet

"That's an unusual pendant you are wearing."

"Yes, it is rather unusual."

"May I look at it?"

"There is really nothing to see."

"Was it a gift?"

"It is something I chose for myself."

"Do you wear it often?"

"Not all the time."

"Why not? It suits you. Don't you like it?"

"Yes, it is one of those things which you need to feel complete."

"But you don't wear it all the time."

"The only item I wear all the time is my watch."

"Are you afraid of being late?"

"Lateness is the other person's problem."

"Is your schedule very pressured?"

"Never really pressured but never really free."

"So what do you like to do in your free time?"

"I like to sleep."

"To sleep! What if someone told you that you had two months free?"

"For two months I would sleep."

"Do you need so much sleep?"

"I like to sleep."

"There must be someone with healing hands that would make you not have to sleep."

"No, I would sleep."

"For two months?"

"I would sleep."

Education

There began the fierce sounds of a house stabbing itself.
However, we were not disposed to listen.
Our attention was transfixed, under the large-scale pine tree,
by a brown bird, quick as dammit, in the dried grass.

Rats have been through my ships. I remember your words:
"Woman is like the wind" – which is poetry,
but makes no sense. That is not the warning,
nor indeed the explanation, given by a friend.

Would you leave your ships to be watched
by the eyes of a mermaid whose hands are gloves
with the fingers broken off, handlers of nothing,
best in museums, the other side of glass?

The blades that back this house are couch grass.
I almost asked to hire a flame thrower.
No use: the roots mat into completeness.
Taking fire as refreshment, how they would spring again.

White as Jasmine

They say, in the family,
usually the women,
though not in whispers,
they say, At this time –
or, At that time –
the same day, the day before,
months or years after someone
died –
a *sweet smell* lingered.
Visiting?
Not a blessing, not a warning.
It is no mystery.
The sweet smell visits the living
in their living place,
never inhabits the dying room.

Why then, in the coach station –
rank oil, ranked taxis,
plastic toys, plastic money,
packed sweat, packed lunches –
Why, then, the smell of jasmine
two days before I
fly home?
Lord white as jasmine,
who has died?
Life is
long in me, lives long before
long after me.
The senses
are too violent
to bear evidence, in this sun
this afternoon,
yet jasmine visits,
strong like evening.

Is it a country has died
within me? Is it
I have died to it, to the past or future
that is my own strange land?

Memory is a professional whisperer.
I smelled a sweet smell.
Who has died?

In Cunaripo

The first time I saw the giant Pandit in his peach-hued kurta,
his whole bulk bespoke his kindness, as he gentled his voice's
    soundwaves
to play with his terrified baby nephew (himself large for his age –
some time after, other children would run away, take fright in
    their turn,
when the big little one cooed down at them, gently proffering
    his toys);
so, what happened with the caymans was entirely in character.

It was the family night
of a festival day.
They opened the door.
Sporting in the ravine
maybe a dozen
baby caymans
and their pianolength mother.
Alligator laughter
splashing and boiling
through their proper element,
sparking off water.
No happier sight.

He scattered consecrated sweets to the beasts,
and the little wedgemouths, delighted, gave chase.
(The mother ignored him, however.) He admired them feasting,
how human and animal could live so close.

Who knows why
he filled in the ravine
later that year,
when he decided
to earth it up.
It is doubtful they died.
Their preferred method
of getting through drought weather

is to be dried into mud.
And even if they did,
who knows how they're reborn.
What a chance. After such blessed food,
perhaps they live in India.
Perhaps they are kalarippayattu masters.

Was it since one small cayman, jagged-jawed, lunged, backed off,
      lunged, backed off,
at his beautiful daughter, when she went out to see to the
      flowers?
Not necessarily.
Should you agree blood is thicker than water.

For Dhumavati: Her Work

Dhumavati is one of the Mahavidyas, aspects of the Hindu understanding of the Absolute as Goddess. She is portrayed as a widow, usually old, ugly, inauspicious, and highly dangerous to those who are not single or detached from the world. She is generous to those who love her. She rejoices in smoke, and partakes of its form.

coil, sated

The sky is digesting
                packed and processing
intestine clouds

coil, grimacing

                grey-white like goathair, like
                worm-white explosions, like
                scar-white fermented milk,
                pyre-white as widow-smoke

coil, gorging

        involvement of clouds
                there is no dispersing
        The sky is digesting war

Welcome, ruin. Mistakeable, ravening.
(war)

Elsewhere in the earth the world is gutted.
Death in the form of death in the form of
A kind of rain feeds the earth.
From the wrinkle of rocks, bird-faced beings
Emerge with a clutch and a rush, taken over
By drinking of blood, sight unseen.

So many lives are countless,
and all eat sounds into beautiful.
(war)

this phantom observing
sun-blind to substance
light behind breakdown
     Lie back and watch,
untransparent breakdown
safe as houses
the sky bellies over
          that use decorum
to restrict the placement of their panes of glass.
this phantom in observance of
Welcome, ruin. Mistakeable, ravening.
(war)
            war.

A Sense of Vanishing

Catch of the Day

Declare the sea unfit
to have had children.
The beaches are the brink of toleration.

The white staircase
meant to lead to the beaches
with a ninety-degree landing

The white staircase
is too swept up
investigating the pull on its ankle

(there are the champagne ruffles,
where is the swell of a hand?)
to seem to invite descent.

No-one bothers to lock
the white staircase
at night; why lock against fools?

Only fools wager a lifetime
which is the wager at an entrance which has been their descent.

II. UNRUFFLED SURFACE

Do you also know some girl,
brilliant, eh, but very much in love,
who sits on the shore real white sand shore,
looking across the crushed-ice and oil-painting water,
the semiprecious-stone improbable colours,
sunned and alert to the sea's gorgeous proceedings
stormed down somewhere else so a near-nylon softness
pervades this bay and this bay alone without a wave?
And you know why the tears are running down her face,
and why there's a change in the way that she sits and will not
        move,
looking at something near like it's playing at being far,
like she never agreed to play and cannot call out game over,
as this cold ocean sea comes up with a setting gelatine swell to
        cover –
still no wave, just a swell, pulling under – clear and unhelped,
        the bright girl's lover –
Yes it is true sometimes. Not recently. I know someone who
        knows her.
Yes it is true always. Out for what it can get. The sea. It has
        nothing to prove.

III. Once Joined to the Mainland

At the tip of the island are islands.

Mapped, it is a flattened boot
cast off by allconquering muscle.

Scraps of leather of metal
strand and button and buckle
in the process of being kicked off
a scrape a scuff a dehiscence
in the nature of speeded-up time
the plan that flattens each tooth

These are the islands that finish the island.

Nowadays the coastguard shoot
smugglers hispanohablantes in pirogues.
Though without that
the tug of the currents that frill out
like dragons, as fresh and as plentiful
as shark, adept at detaching
outer from inner from under,
is dangerous enough. Serpent-mouth

The small islands of a small island have their uses.

Gasparee, Chacachacare, Carrera.
Tourism, leper colony, maximum-penalty prison.

iv. Stop: Warning: Danger: Valentine

It was with memories of Germany
that in every new homeland
she built a red garden
red right through the calendar
a régime of roses, peonies, tulips,
and also the flagstones, the summer umbrellas,
the consolation of meats grilled next to the patio,
the swanning uprightness of promenades with the neighbours.

The sun is setting by the poolside and it is out of season
for red poinsettia, though the crimson anthuriums are present,
and fruit punch is pink with is it grenadine and guava
and a maraschino cherry on the straw she sips through, with the
        sun
blushing at her bare shoulders that are in their fifties, and
        foreign,
and not sure that they can take another holiday burn.
The house prices in the newspaper are too high for paradise.
Her husband's colleagues bought theirs in the eighties. It was
        better then.

Shapes are repeated throughout nature, seldom their meanings.
She does not use grape scissors
because the wracked grape-stems resemble that seaweed
with the berries that popped like vesicles, and pleased her.

The skin on her arms is peeling,
the first sign of fungus
that will work as open as surf
which from second to second manœuvres
flinging between red flags
like lace shown off by a seller
hmmm, the constant replanting of flags
by the lifeguards, repositioning bathers

Inscription (Windward Isles)

By the light that the absorbed Rastafarian carver
said to put inside the calabash lantern
so the pattern comes out
animal, vegetable, abstract,
the twenty questions of this habitat
incised by his mineral edge, to his mind,

I will name them as if you know them,
name locales as if you ought to know them.
. . .
Except that Fort James brings out the suicide in me,
with the part-coral cliffs eroding fast beneath me,
the cave-paths to the Arawak reservoir beneath that, lost,
with the Atlantic roofridges over death below me,
and each and every point disputed, pirated, re-titled,
and the cherished girl's mystery tombstone at my back:
"What was remarkable of her
she was a mother without knowing it
and a wife without letting her husband know it except by her
        kind indulgences to him."
Twenty-one years. Mrs. Betty Stivens. 1783.
And I think of an idiot given in marriage,
not of the innocent, charged with adultery;
not of a slave, or a sailor's good wife;
not of my mother's innocuous vision
of a girl, round-faced and blonde,
seated on a bench near to a tree.
Lux æterna.

Port-of-Spain

A lighthouse that once did what lighthouses do
Now stands towards the middle of town,
For the changes in the shore
And the land that was reclaimed
Made the only Gulf I knew,
The gulf I could not learn to draw.

So much had to be taken back, in those days,
Reclaiming land was taken as read.
(Though the sea alone could lay
Claim to *reclaim* surplus land,
Swallowing the earth's vast wastes).
I did not think the phrase was strange.

None of this explains the dream my mother had,
A dream I shared, not knowing it hers,
Till afterwards. The sea stands.
The sea makes a decision.
The sea arrives, overland.
Sky and wind and ground have lost their rhythm.

The lighthouse stays like the upside-down !
Signalling a Spanish exclamation.
It reminds us we are owned.
Saline makes health safe for us.
And the body, when it's moved,
Weeps its rent in liquid salts.

The Stars Looked Different There

Nothing Poem

I

The first snow has fallen late like the beginning of things
that start without hope of ending, nor do they intend
self-expression. In full day it just lies there. Lesser light
rids its blankness of symbols, brings it to brilliance. Reflect:
Is the opposite of remembrance forgetfulness?
Tall conifers are deepened with it, laurels take a shine,
made most themselves beneath this burden without
     permanence.
Nothing festooned with sheer unlikeness is whited out:
cold clumps raise the mark of the wind-cracked fence, the
     patterned drive
surprises, with its single track of footprints, how long,
how even, the strides. No: hard and soft pass without loss
into each other: distance not to be surpassed is used
to return the power of detail. – The temperature has dropped,
I walk with face uncovered, blood responds with summer bursts,
redness. The freezing air makes an instrument of, finds out,
the throat that ignores its breathing and now owns a thirst, a
     thirst.

II

Wake to a blue that vanishes steadily upwards.
Curtains might as well be pillars, dawn gives their bleakness
such support. This room opening east like a temple
holds only one horizontal in its nothing shape.
Legs are sandbagged. Do not try to sit upright. Substance
punishes the lower half. The upper husks apart
at mere thought of uprights, insect starved out to silver,
fossil of a shadow torso, cage hinged on a puff of smoke.
Just as the orchard's remnant rejects young-old branches
powdered green on black by damp – unwholesome firewood –
sleep should reject as a start this budding consciousness,
break from the day to come, sink again, truly archaic.
Sleep plucks for the attention of a figure in a cloak,
whose hair is in soft movement, as pure as oxygen,
but whose command of vertigo is greater. Not death,
you say; and, be reassured, not love. Now make the leap.

III

I insist that you will be another of the nothing figures,
that you will be one more, that you will stay, uncommunicated,
that there is something significant for me to withhold in you.
To make it difficult, unclassifiable enough a gift –
that new, that much more fastidious, resistant flower-structure –
Not one crystallographer – perhaps a marine biologist –
would do, could engineer it so it was not fatal, not mortal –
your image taken into the blue, into the unheralded,
repetitious, lost-messenger, the height-without-lift, depth-
        without-
perception blue. A wedge of coral, bone-white, spotted with
        heartsblood,
makes hard sense only since worked around unbreathing
        crannies, since form's
exaction by vivid pockets that let life run out from where it
        lived.
As if by accidents, whole coasts are pink with it: the colour of
cruelty, also of dilution, worn fine through generations
from tide to tide. This bloom is like that: unkind and
        unpretending,
at each point seeming limitless, grained and ablaze. Have it from
        me.

IV

One hundred and fifty degrees of pain is all
most can manage. More, further, further, I would move
me away – become the diameter in all
directions, leave unbelieving – the element
of randomness acquires a half-life, is gone,
like all else reacting upon you, is gone. Now
the radiance having nothing to do with health,
adapting all time, digits on dials wiped clean,
that is it, cursed exaggeration of an act
that clocks a never having been. Desire offends
all objects. An ill-timed touch on a mass suspended
above the one doorway that singles out daylight
starts wrongness: grim points, massive in broken rotation,
swing into wild injury: crush headlong: superb,
as when fear's half-circles round off to hate; unchoosing.
This is total for the moment – too late – prolonged –

Time is an Unkind Dancer

Climacteric

Your story is twice-folded. Medicine induced
a saving menopause, once you were cut and hurt
to clear away the discord which produced itself
inside you, sickest spontaneity. Tides
are reversed, and knowledge overpowers you, full
yet preliminary, in process. You were aged,
and are returning, and will in nature age again,
pressured to beauty. At present, have your
meanwhile – your doubled year recovering
a subtler south.

Beauty. 'She earned that face.' They say
that, when a star turns thirty. Drying-out
bequeaths her cheekbones; steel weights
have fanned her swanning, aspirational neck.
But you – you have not earned *that* face. No,
you deserve serenity, the drizzled stresses
wisdom scans through youth. Look, how
your heightened skeleton pulls flesh into
transparencies, wearing ahead of time and
gravity! You work like that, drawing old lines
of music from among the ins and outs of
scribe and image, when you edit vellum
furred with light.

Motets will run like mirror for you, back and forth.

Turning Moment

I

The air begins to flow with darkness.
Like a sleeve that, cracking the air, is filled with force,
Among the corona of lines that is the body's extension of force,
Light's positive opposite engenders us.
See, the inanimate grows dim
And loses ground?
We sharpen,
Widen, composing a grid of rays,
That is the sense of, sense beyond, our substance.
The movement of a voice springs weaponed, higher than speech,
To space that meets a space never to close with speech.
Can reality outdo its own encounter?

II

So fast, all around us,
    where is it,

cloud of cloths, whirl of sails,
high-velocity theme?

Not safe, no speed limit
    on dreaming

Fatalities turn in such sleep.

III

Autumn, the poisoned landscape, and impossible you:
Nothing to buy for who would or could consume:
Inedible berries redden on private trees –
Streets narrow, streets widen, tricked in greys –
Cold travels in too slowly. How not want
Winter's accelerations, unfinished and expert.

IV

Grip to crunching, seize
without break, feather-lightening jeweller. Strike,
move, remove,
                facet it
in four dimensions,
my brilliant of pain.

What is real, and so
white and blue and dark, red, at once.

Eat into jaw, living scimitar.
So shine, threadless ivory, for the shelf.

Grapple marble teeth
out of mind, jar them – yours?
This, then,
                in isolation
is without
a kind of grief.

White Lilac Time

The path so thick with leaves it seems a stream
The stream so thick with weeds they net like grass

Do not believe it was technical need
that exposes the gaze in old photographs,
the half minute living without blinking
the ancient camera stipulated.
Floodlit points into a cavern through a graph
still are found under unexpected brows,
dejected, seated piercingly, clubbed insane,
posed in original space on public paths.

Best resign lost sight, draw back, since this bridge
Is hinged only on one side, walk away

Research routinely says the colour green
relaxes. Conifers are common planting,
not needing care. Precision pinecones scatter,
requiring too complex focus, on our way
to work. Magic makes no exceptions, it is
unsympathetic. The wait for the search
for the cure of the wound in the cause of
the wound cross-hatches the wound's own renewal.

The path so thick with leaves it seems a stream
The stream so thick with weeds they net like grass

It does not follow, that the sun
Moves, it does not follow.

She moves through her thinking room and
Through, finding no shadow.

The city holds what it does not know
Scorched from all sides

In the inconsistent arch of trees
Light solidifies

Best resign lost sight, draw back, since this bridge
Is hinged only on one side, walk away

Likes loves wants misses, lyrical, she – someday –
might even need. This house of cards alive
with novel suits plays no-solution patience
as regards an upturned face. Quote, unquote,
the idea, in absence, can almost exceed
what for the moment happiness believes, while
presence withheld retains the upper hand
beyond understanding happiness explained.

The staring path so hot it locked in song
The staring path so hot it locked in song
The pulsar song so hot it started dark
The pulsar song so hot it started dark

Miss Havisham Will Not Burn

Only if you are one of those who read the novel,
followed the slug-frosting canal where rats scuffle,
crafts shuffle, like the unforgiving face-cards of the deck
you have trousered as a talisman against dismissal, knave or jack
worth one point towards game; one point
as a trump; three points if Jack of Trumps gets hanged.

Even you may come too late, inexcusable reader,
without the catching castor taste for how objects are lit by
        darkness,
transmitters of a palpable Touch-me-not. Isn't it acquired,
like the taste for foie gras, the pâté of a richness that burrows
sparingly into its jar, paste of some wretched and over-rich
geese buried up to their necks, livers enlarged like an idealist's
        sorrows.

Not that, if you come, they can provide any refreshment;
none beyond the solid heartbreaks on perspective
(pure grey where you expect a greenish termination to the
        spectrum)
of sash windows outside history, genuinely old glass,
solid as water banked by Thames upon a pregnant corpse,
filtering you into the conversation of centuries with lads-upon-
        the-leash.

Many have come for the cake. You are merely the latest,
in this place where remarks have hardened like fluids, to pick up
a milk-delicate teacup webbed over
with an old lace of spider-secretions; vehement saliva;
tear-drops passed like mucus, traceable by the fingers,
leaving the eye alone to its ironies; and who knows what others.

(She goes around and around the room, like a river
run underground among stalactites; cold herself, like a river
whose tributaries all have been earthed up, diverted,
dry-bedded, built over, each and every spring been dammed.
Suddenly you are paper. On the oak table, a place-card with your
      name.
Do you fall into step. Was the game always Catch as Catch Can.)

You failed to notice it, having imagined that it had to be gothic:
since they said "wedding", a cathedral base to spires
in moulded royal icing, perhaps with ivy encrustations on the
      sides?
White it was, certainly, and not much gone:
tier on tier, raised by simple equations, decked with orange
      blossom,
the oblongs diminish, an ascent of coffins for Russian dolls.

Light and Dark

"On a planet where the sun rises
just once every six months,
light, in its slightest manifestation,
will be worshipped – will it not?

"The tiniest sequin reflector,
minute pinhead matchsticks,
the devices, the receptacles,
for any kind of flame –
they would be precious, shy, expensive.
Birthday lamps would be few
but large, and unspeakably gorgeous.
The words of love, the name of friendship,
all would be gifts of light – ?"

"No.

"Total and absolute is the love
of darkness. Light achieves
no more than clarity – not even;
it blurs, without solving.

"With what passionate serenity
the adherents of dark
cut that world's bare wind with their faces!
Their work is like dancing.
It is the stretch when the tear has healed,
dark, the home after time,
it is the calm where monsters are safe
to move one limb every million years
to finish their embrace."

Though,
as a matter of fact, on that planet
the sun is taboo. The trade
in contraband lamps,

re-jigged leaking batteries,
black-market torches,
all sorts, is exorbitant.
Matches are cruelly taxed.
The level of theft is high.
Pearl-finish cigarette lighters
are built with a flick-knife component.
The keeping of pets is forbidden.
The hoarding of tallow is rife.

Therefore
the second speaker was punished
in the sense saturation chamber.
Brilliance on brilliance destroyed her
as, laid out like a starfish,
she smiled from her vanishing eyepoints
as if their visions were reconciled.

Obsessive Talk

Twist

I

Focused blade-rotating circulation locust buzz
drives into cores reproaches leakage, faultiness,
amplifies intensifies churrs powers winds inside
(put awash with faultiness with leakage lolling head)
my head a flooded street with swimming geese, inlaid
with fixity of nothing nothing but a spreading lid
tile-crazy like an icesheet knapped by puzzling residue.
Toiling plates at earthscale crack unseeably. The moon
appears, an aztec moon, tethers haloes over storm
skittering with scarlet energy. Exhale, go on,
sort out what, like lead, is densest, what will not break down.
The moon appears to know what it is doing, what I did.

II

I dreamed I was growing red roses, those troublesome flowers
that repay for such flitting time (months briefed by coldness)
pains taken, the heft of the spade and the heaviest buckets –
staked roses holding themselves unbeholden,
no nodding to even the appearance of care.

What I would say is dripping and knotting, like a gold chain
       neglected
so the flow of its links sets to fighting and mating
in deadlock, the art of its clasp now securing no purpose –
a thing not for wearing nor for discarding,
to shine light no longer, absorbed in a box.

What you will not see is that there is no telling –
in the rite of avoidance there is no more hunting,
the reflex an end in its push-away self like an infix
that brackets words to annulment – the most forward objects
by the mind's eye already have been reinverted.

III

I am the last thing you would want to see in the morning.
I am the bare roof of a house whose birds have been put to flight
    or slaughtered.
I am taffeta that takes the floor, pirouettes, with no body to
    support it.
I am not for waking to at night.

What's a wolf, it's a scavenger, thirsting in moonlight,
pitched out of your civil calendar, thirteen months scything
    prime across twelve.
No matter the distance, if you'd (yellow for danger) the sense
    alive to know me,
I'd sink my teeth in your unbelief.

Your social smile is pathetic, indifferent and floral.
You flicker in and out of happiness as if sufficiency were usual.
You're seashell-pink and pale with being almost perfection, more
    frail than the normal.
Have you the design to be my kill.

IV

A cypress is growing inside me.
It lifts me up to cry
plastered on damask in armchairs.
It makes you tired, too.

A cypress is permanent in me.
I cannot answer when
temperature's evidence alters.
I saw no where but in.

The Monster Scrapbook

My dear J.,

Very many thanks for the box of Lapsang. It brings back strangely comforting memories of your den, where the smells of tea, smoke, old books and new slippers commingle. Though, dear lad, I have to say that a trip to the dry cleaners' will do no harm whatsoever to that dressing gown of yours. I am not to be persuaded that the hue of said dressing gown originally was black, nor that its colour has deepened to match your moods. I can hear your short laugh of objection as if I were once again in that villainous leather armchair before your stinking fireplace, with you standing in your characteristic posture at the window, back turned to your interlocutor, letting drop the occasional mordant epigram by way of supposed response, in those intervals of window-gazing when even you must show a sign of life, and knock the ashes out of your tropical purpleheart wood pipe. How goes it, dear fellow? As for myself, I continue much as ever. I have not been down to the docks lately. It's blasted rheumaticky weather, though it is supposed to be that season than which nothing is as beautiful. Spring rain goes straight to your old friend's needs – aha, I was about to write, knees. So here I am, virtuous as a snowdrop, and feeling just as unseasonal.

Seriously, now, old J., I am (as ever) writing to you with the hope of passing a task to your shoulders, that may be half the breadth of mine but are more than wiry enough for the purpose. Do you remember that vexed question, when last the Society convened, as to whether the WOLF or the BEAR is the more powerful follower, familiar, spirit, totem, guide, or what you will, of the Shaman?

Do you not share my instinct, that some among us are most closely akin to those hybrid and marvellous beasts which haunt legend, manuscript, and folk memory alike? Have you never met someone whose fetch seems to have both scales and feathers, like some abominable, or at the very least inedible, apparition dismissed by the sane and sober writers of Leviticus?

Let me assure you that I am myself perfectly sane and sober. A bundle of writings has lately come my way, from (I regret to admit) a family member. Yes – even families that are not Royal have their Monsters. Some later hand has annotated these writings, and done a cut and paste job on them. It is difficult to say how much has been discarded. It is impossible to know whether the lack of method with which the materials have been combined reflects a lack of skill, a lack of interest, the need to conceal a family secret, or the extreme perturbation of spirit into which the compiler was thrown by the horrifying implications of what lay before his eyes. I shall not say, her eyes, for on the topic of Monsters females have little sense, and would doubtless have preserved the documents in their entirety, indeed adding notes of admiration to the bizarreries there contained.

You must have known Monsters. You must have known people whose eyes hit you with large and sudden appeals – people whose capacity for feeling and action seems sometimes more, sometimes less, than the human – people who are ill-treated outrageously by those whom they love, and elevated to positions of esteem and responsibility by those to whom they are indifferent.

They induce SPECIES FEAR, a kind of wincing of the soul (if there is a soul) if you so much as sight them in the street.

The following MONSTER SCRAPBOOK seems to me, taken as a whole, a true image of the MONSTER STATE OF MIND – lacking the Monster scope and the Monster bent, perhaps, but true as to the essence of the experience of Monsterdom.

It consists of highly disparate parts, as do the minds of Monsters (if one may speak of Monsters' minds). It is a feature of the Monster mind that the most abrupt transitions and the unlikeliest effusions are believed by the Monster to connect. Excessive acquaintance with Monsters or the Monster way will lead any reader, except the most robust, to believe in and pursue this Monstrosity of connections. This is why I would suggest the title OBSESSIVE TALK for the finished collection which (excuse the impertinence!) you, my dear J., will have edited. In the meantime, I have left the original compiler's title, THE MONSTER SCRAPBOOK, to stand. It is my belief that even the apparent stretches of prose are to be read as poetry. Monsters want logic, therefore everything they speak is a kind of poem. Your fine mind will assemble in its entirety the continuous poem which is the MONSTER SCRAPBOOK in its ideal state. It requires only your reading – the POEM will stand complete.

Ever yours,

H.

Monster Postures

- Identify Monster Posture most appropriate to occasion
- Assume said Monster Posture
- Begin the Monstrous Task

MONSTER POSTURES

(1) Standing with all four legs on top of a small upturned tub
(2) Tethered balloon
(3) Flat on the floor
(4) Bendy toy that has gone straight
(5) Eighteen inches above top of own head
(6) Falling backwards from the shoulders up, at the top of a staircase on level ground
(7) All of a heap
(8) Frolicsome
(9) Nose pointing
(10) Nose painting
(11) One paw trapped, other paws floppy
(12) Gambolling and gollolloping
(13) In the depths of despair
(14) Extraordinarily careful of multiple tails
(15) Bawling with hunger
(16) Flip the giraffe

Inappropriate Monster Postures have not been given

The Monstrous Task

OF THE CHARACTER OF *MONSTERS*

It grieves Monsters to be treated as if they were hateful strangers.
Friends meet sometimes, talk a little, have a drink, sit quietly.
Then they return to their work, refreshed. Monsters are nervous.
They interrupt people, by trying to engage them in Monster play.
Monsters are nervous because they are much fallen in love with.
People who work fall in love with them, and explain to the
Monsters that they must be fitted in. Monsters are kennelled in
the interstices of other lives. This is not because of *low self-esteem*
or *poor self-image*. Monsters protest. They repudiate the language
of damage and repair. You, for example, are absolutely secure in
your identity as Monster. There are friends who scratch your
rattling scales and nudge little gobs of rank meat towards you. You
play coy about accepting, and get through whole ostriches at one
sitting. Monsters, however, keep pushing the limits. They cosy
up grotesquely to non-Monster-friendly people. They imagine
communion with some ordinary world where people look up, and
smile, and look down again, returning to their work without need-
ing to salute *Monster consciousness*. Monsters, being so much fallen
in love with and therefore nervous, have codified their three pet
fears.

(1) That someone they respect will suddenly start to talk nonsense,
without appearing to notice the transition.

(2) That someone they like will disappear, for nothing that seems
like a reason.

(3) That someone who has glimpsed their sheer Monstrosity will
reject them afterwards, not as friends, but completely, as *a kind
of thing*.

These fears have nothing to do with the commonly held miscon-
ceptions that Monsters are prone to spout absurdities; that they eat

people; and that they invite their friends into their wardrobes to dress them up in Monster Shawls.

You know the strange mildness with which people treat you, because they have reserved the option of leaving you, because you are a Monster. Monsters have developed great finesse in detecting the tones of finality. They sniff finality even before it is inherent in the moment, before it is conscious or intended in anything that anyone has said. This is because Monsters try to learn, but there are things they cannot do by trying. What happens, in the learning process of a Monster, is that they think about what it would be like if they could already do something; for example, hear themselves objectively when they are playing the oboe. Then, one day, while not trying, they find that they have acquired the skill.

You know that Monsters, being fatalistic, have a great love of music. Monster torch songs include: *Round and round the rugged rock the ragged rascal ran, Non sap chantar*, and a great deal that is Scottish.

DESDEMONA RESUSCITATED

Far more unremarkable if she dreamt of him never
but when reminded by a parchment-coloured handkerchief
(lace torn at the corner leaving a gap like asthma
between the shaking cambric body and scarab-hard edge),
nostrils closing to a scent erroneously called jasmine.
Her dream had grown with a difference, less absence than age.

Black sky and black earth cup their hands together, finger to
finger, wrist to stemming wrist. Beyond is irrelevance.
Between is staked a pole. An immensity of fire
plays with that space, without sound. Upon that pole a body,
lower back impaled or supported, a fermata.
Its lowest points face upwards. No external consciousness.

Passage   I must take passage
Across unpredicted ocean
That no-one troubles to find
No-one would take the trouble to find
My new surroundings   I need surroundings
That will be arduous   unalluring
Sea-surrounded.
I can pay for it.
Somewhere with a sun
That touches the equatorial
That makes day and night fast equals
All year round
So noon is always white, so copper means
That dusk in blueness without trembling
Is ninety minutes near,
Except when rain blots out the calendar
And sweet greyness keeps indoors
To mind the house
Sea-surrounded. I can pay for it,
Somewhere with a sun

That makes the land grow easy   without toil
Sun stretching over waking   like contentment
That makes the children look
As if they could be his
Dark   his
Wide-ranging   his
Volatile in brilliance
As if assuredly
His
And mine.
Flight   I must take passage
For health   waxed oranges
Extra linen   make a note of it
And for emergencies
A source of light.
I hear him laugh at these particulars.
I'll take no music.
My skin is tight over his voice.

I cannot do her justice, nor can I let her rest.
You know by now I'd think I saw her anywhere.
Perhaps it would be different in summer circumstances,
because I'd live each summer like her last,
a matter of maintaining unimportant quiet,
things endured, admired, stored, ventured, missed.
Nonetheless

Without energy for elegy

I am everything and nothing

Do not ask me how I know what I know

One of the colours of sleep is lilac

But something shattered me once,
I think,

Something that would not call again.

Sometimes I wanted it, to try again.

Soon I shall be free of her. / Determine her. A standard / For the status of her radiance. / This cannot be how – // I am pinned to the thought of her / like a sheet to a window-frame / (winds roughen) / where the glass has gone / in recent violence. // I'd try to take her measure / as if holding to the light / clear liquid in a beaker, / steadying my eye on the / meniscus, the imagined / line underpinning surface / curve. I can't approximate, // save myself from the thought of her. / Make it a shape, like the matt flow / of an unglazed vase. At every throw, / what I scarcely choose to call her / soul makes an appearance, a flaw, / sunders the body – thinning it – / from perfectibility, while / realigning the light to / perfection. I can see it now. //

Again she petrifies me with her change.
Frail, frail, and walking slowly as the dawn,
She wrinkles, falls to shining. Out of range,
I stand in that walled square. Height seems to turn,
And exits flicker with it. All is gone,
Of neither fixed nor followed dailiness,
Except the stonework. That is monotone.
She leaves me nothing. Hence her endlessness.
Trapped in a rhomb of ice a chainmail carp's
A gleam beneath my sinking English moon,
Off-centre in the fountain. Legend sharps
These non-encounters. Time resumes me then.
I speak of her too often – look, before
I cannot recognise her any more.

This is easy. To gain the trust of a Monster, all you have to do is to speak to it three times a month or so, in human language, with reference to biscuits. Trust is not necessary as a first step in Monster deception, however. To deceive a Monster, you merely have to invent, or suspect, some kind of scene. Then, declare a real disbelief in this scene. The intensity of your declaration of disbelief will irresistibly fascinate the Monster. It is irrelevant, and also impossible to ascertain, whether the Monster does come to believe in your scene. What matters is that the Monster will become obsessed with, even tormented by, your scene as a possibility.

It is important to cultivate a schematic lack of self-knowledge, if you wish to become a Class A Monster deceiver. A good exercise is to hold open possibilities that could easily be resolved. If you insist enough on holding these possibilities open, you may become genuinely unable to decide for one or the other. The next step is to present the unresolved possibilities to a Monster in such a way that the Monster cannot bear the tension which you yourself ought to (but don't) feel, under these uncertain conditions. The Monster will rush to formulate a question. The Monster will rush to resolve the question. The Monster, honourable by long practice rather than by nature, will thereafter adhere to one or the other of the possibilities with which you have presented it. You do not have to present one of the alternatives favourably. You merely have to make the tension unbearable to the Monster mind. Begin your practice on a slow Monster (though these can be tenacious, not to say glutinous), until you are expert in setting out possibilities by which the Monster is sure to lose in a way that sufficiently entertains you.

I'm not very fond of narrative continuity
in visual media.

The capped I the pillar, the dotted i
the pinhead. Civilization and the solitary,
one not requiring witness, the other unsure
of record.

In the news today: the Neanderthals
made superglue.

Seeing Without Looking

Imagine three things.

First, a set of printed stanzas: a song. The music for the words is printed beneath the stanzas, a patterned horizontal that under-girds the long column of language. You hear the words spoken. The voice in your head refuses to linger. The words are spoken, recited, not chanted, just faintly coloured by their knowledge of their own potential for rapture. The visible scoring of music seems to move beneath the stanzas, not heard, but punctuating the spoken song, like the pause at the back of the wind before it restarts its hollow speech, if you are a careful listener with ears attuned to the conditions prevailing at the feet of mountains. All this is in the mind.

It is as if you were a visitor to some old place that has a significance that you are not equipped to apprehend. You turn your head, to catch a gleam on the glass, and a fit of movement that could be in the long room or could be a reflection of one of the trees beyond the terrace from which you have just turned away your head. You stay out on the terrace, unsure of the source of the gleam, whether in the woods in front and beyond you, or in the long windowed room of the house which you do not much care to re-enter.

Second, a page of printed music: a song. The words for it are printed underneath, running along with the notes, and they appear diminished, being stretched, compressed, dividing and resuming according to the strict lines which the printed music has fixed. The place of the words is dependent. It is secondary. It is intermittent. Special attention has to be paid to notice that the words have a continuous logic of their own. Without special attention, you notice them from time to time, which is to say that you fail to notice their stanzaic nature at all. You hear the music. Below that, there seems to be a stir of language. Something wants to be communicated. But the articulations of language are, as much as anything, a series of stops. The music does not stop. It continues across its pauses, each of which is a four-dimensional encounter, each encounter being a miracle of containment. The music in your head is what you hear, in the way that you can tell the distribution of clouds by the succession of soft greyness and white light framed by the oblong of your window, a pattern that holds your attention whether or not it has your attention. All this is in the mind.

It is like remembering somebody whom you dreamed, someone whom you never knew, someone who (as far as you can know) has no existence beyond what you have dreamed. The pain that comes with the waking realization that this memory belongs to imagination is dumb. It baffles the experience of bereavement. You truly sorrow that you will never meet the person you have never met. Perhaps the details of the dream are historical. Still, the face is too particular. It holds the meaning which can make portrait galleries uneasy places. Beside the unknowns and the idealizations, this is the person-in-storage, the one portrait that is not, should, cannot be there.

Third, a page of lyrics and music: a song. This is how it is set out. There are three staves. The top stave bears the melody, with the words running underneath, printed in the space between this and the two instrumental staves. You would like to rationalize it as a grid. No, the effect is of parallelisms, of things that are separate yet that are, in so far as they become ultimate, irretrievably enmeshed. You are standing in the rain with your eyes closed, feeling the gravity of downward water pulled across you by the direction of the wind. All this is in the mind.

This is the song that starts up when life has retreated to the edges of a place kept desolate and majestic. This is the tune for the figure in the long room and on the terrace, the one not in the portraits. It is not safe, it is more than museums.

IN THE LOFT

Watching the mouthwatering dawn
break, dawn, fleecy and remote,
no deceptions about its power.

Dawn broke like the proverbial butterfly on
a wheel. Day itself seemed to have a difficulty
with the idea of waking up in this country.

damn the transition
from the girls i was
to a giggling venus
using men
in a hard case

i'll break the butterfly
before they can catch it
while they're still playing
at being limp-wristed
oh the surprise

X. turns to face you. There is a big smile on his face, so big that it seems to be pushing at his eyes. He had turned his back while removing the many layers of his navy, burgundy, fawn and white English tailored, knitted, woven clothing, some rough, some fine in texture, all expensive. He had arranged them neatly, like items for parcel post to family abroad, on the right-hand ledge of the second-hand walnut veneer dresser.

His white underwear looks big to match his smile, and absurd. You think of diapers. There are TV documentaries on German men (why German men?) who go to brothels to be babied.

Suddenly his face lengthens. His eyes begin to stare. His mouth goes small. Sunlight is velveting the tended gloss and pile of his skin. The large window is uncurtained. It is late spring. The remains of an orchard and the remains of woodland: apple and horse chestnut trees: being old, have stayed near leafless.

Suddenly he is at you. It is a nasty playground rush, both arms held out in front of him. Such stiffness. You are sitting on the edge of the futon mattress (frameless by choice), your feet tucked onto the floor.

The waist of the trousers is seized in two hands. It is tugged downwards, regardless of fastenings or the shape or posture of the woman's body. He does a half-jump backwards – bafflement. The wasp-coloured light that played around his face, gratified in anticipation, does not go out. It notches itself into a glare of petulant ferocity. Both hands drop to his sides. He stands. His gaze rebukes you. It makes the most of the drop down in height caused by where you have placed yourself.

Tired of feeling childish, you resignedly demonstrate the ends of the drawstring that runs through the lightweight fabric.

The rebuking gaze continues. His tended hair flops forwards. The face looks drawn in about the nose.

Still silence.

You undo them yourself.

AND AGAIN

I

I must have told you, I met the
neighbours? I think they're our age,
but they have children. He seemed much
nicer. Sweeping the driveway.
Stopped & asked me in. Don't know what
he *does.* She's not so relaxed.
I think, three children – oh, maybe
nine seven & two? Girls. Blonde –
it seems amazingly normal,
hereabouts. They are *local*:
for generations, only moved
village. It's incestuous.
She's not very blonde. – Country life
is odd; I couldn't believe – !
My shoes are useless. There are no
street lights.
        I was unfriendly, I suppose,
to her. She's on my conscience.
It's never easy.
        People live around & for their
houses. Always doing things.
It's quite frightening.
        She's solid. Uncomfortably.
Dissatisfaction has dried
into her. She kept on joking
about her dullness, as if
she wanted a readymade friend.
I did not want her to get
to know me & speak for hours
on the telephone. It gets
so – sticky. Time bleeding from me.
– I get so frantic when I'm off
the pill.

II

I never watch the news,
the night before another
supermarket trip is due.
Not why you think. It's not
the cruelty. It's not
the animals who body
guilt & personality,
reminding me in every joint
that floppy toys are sold
as tokens
of propitiation. &
my tea leaves never form
a skinny foot. I can't
afford to bother
about blood.
Ask the Jain: with simple
breath, we kill.
  It is the labels. They
can terrify.
A superhuman code,
delaying choice, because
they face me with our
ignorance, their level
promise over com-
promise.
  I'd cope much better if I'd
been brought up religious,
fitting dreams round crevasses.
  Organic oranges are
squashier. A good thing,
surely? well it is
for me.

III

I don't think dreams can
say much. No more than skelping
surface, while the processing
machine leaves us its by-products
in the dark. Listen:
    I was with you last night,
in a classroom situation.
You were the teacher. One long window
to the right, the east, & light
was failing in the room, the light
came through, diminishing.
    When I was younger,
two mirrors – turned so I could fix
both my profiles & my back –
went green from one another,
reflected in each other
with just such loss of light.
Something like that, & sometimes
more like being under willows.
    We were alone,
except that on the desks were
steaks, one per desk, like stand-ins:
ruby, dumb & quivering
as if no heat or pressure,
no extreme would change their life
to normal substance. Somehow
in the dream we could ignore
that meat, & get on with our
talking.
    – Never mind all that.
"Good news, bad news." Which one first? –
A woman at the bus stop

said the roadworks were because
the soil there needs replacing.
Arsenic, mercury &
lead. They found it when a house
was being built. Her face was red
& puffy. No-one's building
here, so *they* won't test our soil.
& the good news? – Better late
than never: *it* was waiting
for the moon, I suppose.

IV

All the daffodils
are out in the border, some
drooping already, they get
blowzy so quickly, their scent's
pale & powdery.
    They remind me
of something I wanted – or
something I want to forget.
    So. Buy flowers
for the house, lace curtains,
spruce the place up.
    That sky! Like winter skin –
like good skin you don't care for –
it gleams, anyway! Till spring,
trees are private, like hair.
    I think you'd love this dress.
I picked it up this morning
for a song – the violet's
not too intense – but see,
it's bleached or streaked a little,
on the straps – I wouldn't say
it was a flaw – perhaps it runs,
mind. Rinse it in cold water.
It's pleated like a dancer's.
    I'll dampen it &
twist it, knotting up the ends –
the pleats will tighten, so they
shimmer.
    I dare say it will take
quite some time to dry. It must
be wrung out hard.
    I think of
you – without a use – for me.

IN THE LOFT

Elle qui sait être seule
Emma of the bells of Florence
Elle qui sait être seule
Emma of the glass of Ireland
Elle qui sait être seule
Emma of the West Country

Monster Pastimes

If asked, they will say that they like to sleep. Monsters, however, are great readers. Their reactions to poems are written up in purple. Monster underpasses and Monster school walls, Monster public bathrooms and Monster slums have uncritical rhapsodies instead of personal or political graffiti. Like so much graffiti, Monster purple prose manages to be simultaneously opaque and effaced.

Monsters get lost in their own poems. These poems are solid on the page, lovingly carved blocks in a sculpture park of ruins. They are severely refashioned by weathering. Light is let through between their lines. Monsters live among poems. It is their commonplace. They walk among poems all day, listening to the hard wind, and taking the stones quite for granted. They forget that the poems are not geological formations. The interior landscape of Monsters would seem, but only seem, to be composed of rocks that had pushed up or tumbled in great, long past movements, during the foundation of the place where the Monsters brood. The Monsters brood over the creative geography of poems as if they had to put together a map.

Monsters brooding over internal speech dog the footsteps of their friends, and insist on speaking in ellipses. They mouth each ellipsis as if it were something newly caught, not as if something were left out. Monsters in this state are memorable, but not striking. They verge on not being Monsters at all. Listening to the externalizations of their buried speech is like experiencing a condition. You do not find anything to say in return. Monsters fall silent, turning away from adequate communication, as if it were only intermittently bearable to their physical form. Monsters wallow and skim when they wish to be at their most condensed. They live gracelessly, at ground level.

I Hear the Monsters Singing

Radiance of daylily dromedaries
Argument by allegation of seagulls
Vertical termagant curtain
Eucalyptus syrup calipers alligators
Hellebore – palisade – nightgown,
Everready treadmill, instil bravado.
Forceps. Concepts. Conch-shells. Precepts, prefects.
Bougainvillæa vervain bovine gorgonzola extravaganza ample.

Coalpot clothespin cut cloth compost
Tingling igloo tickling tinkling inking tintinnabulation chink

Backtracking timekeeping fingersnapping (make it snappy) happyclappy
  triggerhappy
Happening apenas de veras acanthus replenish disrelish

Parang microphone hareng lycra tired-out warrahoon
Quaquaversal. Quaquaversally. Henry Roy.

CHARM

He said *Thank you*, his unbraced smile glittering,
making the supporting air suddenly ponderous,
as if heavy with halted – halted, more than impending –
snow. He said *Thank you*; his eyes neither on her
nor the object, fixed on the occasional form of
this occasion (beside the question
whether non-event). She felt offended and felt
apart from being offended surprised at the
taking of offence. She felt as printed words
might react if they could overhear, could realize,
that the theorist had used them to praise the
silence between the lines.

MONSTER FLATTERY

Monsters are flattered if you accuse them. They fall in love with you if you insult them. They have a thing for archaic language. 'Dissembling cub' is a term of abuse that never fails to melt them. The flattered Monster will turn to you, then a little away from you, then to you again, scrutinizing you, all the darkness of the Monster's features lightening from distrust and disappointment to distrust and doubt, then distrust and hope, at last beyond hope, fully open into trust. During this time, if you wish to hook your Monster properly, ignore it, and keep talking to other, preferably human, interlocutors.

LUX ÆTERNA ET PERPETUA

It is suddenly so much easier to create the sharp-edged forms of beauty, falling like a shadow over everything else but at little cost.

Looking at my garden I know that iris sibirica must come up like a sword from the earth and that trailing rosemary should be a green wave fixed in its rush towards the paving stones. It takes no planning, now.

I inhabit the place in my mind so fully that my imagination sees it as it must best be; more and more we mirror one another, I fear that in this suburb I am putting down roots.

Passing from a city to which you had moved, into a city where you never mean to live, then into the place of departures, where you do not hope that anyone may coincide, what there is to look forward to is your sole transfer once more to time zones shared by some other set of friends, time zones a thousand-odd miles remote from each other yet letting us perhaps dream in tandem, if intuition is ever a reliable guide. To tap through the same hours as friends once more, now less, remote, is an absence from absence.

What are you talking about?
      The onset.
Why make the crying-out, the chasing-after,
      They have gone too far?
Watch it. Watch it.
      The outset.
Hobble them. Ribbon them.
      You have come a long way,
considering. Considering,
Haven't we done well.

The tentative body instinct with the speaking mind. No excess of music suffices. The mind at once cleaves and brightens and the body with it, like a wooden stave-church whose steeple, struck by lightning, conducting a fire that immolates as it outlines, exposes, finally makes sense of the timber frame that held together the opaque building meant to contain the silence of collective sounds. The conjunction of rite and meaning must be as hot, bright, and terminal as this.

Is it so terrible to be asked, "What is it?" Would you mean it if you said it? If I could say it I could only say it as if I did not mean it. If you could say it it would be as if you did not mean it. In which case . . . I always have time for you once you invent a reason. But, truth is, if it were possible for you to tell me about this thing, I don't know how it would be, I wouldn't know how to be. It has been guarded so long, most particularly against us, it is every day, how to bring it into the everyday. (Bacchus to Pentheus. Ah! as the god says, when the man would hear those things which are bitter to him. Cue transvestism, wild women, and dismemberment.)

Lactic Song

still
tiger pause
no
tiger paws

the loon rises monosyllabic in a eunuch sky

still
primrose feint
no
primrose faint

violin salix yields up blades sawing in a dorsal swoon

the hunger laid in heaps by roots
crescents crooning mahonia
the regular envoicing fox
gurgles in deft jugular

the flood delivers crocodiles to the yardlong porch

still
keen the wring
not
yammer ring

the horse bays for its measuring stick admired in astral school

not
keen the words
still
yammer sword

In love with loving, they love beside themselves for years and decades, which is very ageing. The equilibrium they find still has its part in a quiet upset. They have allowed themselves to suffer into the idea of being in love with others, even the act of it, and though this was not factitious, and though it was extreme, it had the quality of being an inessential. When they can no longer deal with inessentials, age is stripping them. They no longer feel anything of anything. Isolate creatures, they insist on a yearning to hear their own voices again exercising those tones – tones fetched from a distance, low but even on the breath – that cannot be produced to order, and which sound fatuous in description. They conceive of themselves as instruments encased, ornamental on the wall, sounding-boards stiffening into monotones. They have tried to fall in love with other people, and to leave the idea of The One alone. This idea has resisted reason. It persists like a tiredness in the heart muscle, like a growing pain in the bones. So much negative energy has propelled them. What would the strength of it be if indeed it could run clear? The thing about them is that they have never been too young, not as someone else might have been too young.

Stop-looking-at-me-your-eyes-are-too-bright-they-will-burn-a-hole-through-me-they-will-leave-my-skull-a-fishingnet-of-ivory-my-skeleton-reduced-and-useless-a-lace-fringe-of-seafoam-bone.

"I cannot believe that there was ever a time when I did not know you." That is the kind of thing which lovers are supposed to say to one another. That is what they are supposed to aspire to want to mean. This is seldom, if ever, true of actual lovers, who, at the stage when they are supposed to make these pretty observations, tend instead to flip between setting up a monstrous distance between one another, and removing themselves utterly from the unideal presence of the beloved. "I cannot believe that there was ever a time when I did not know you," is a truth continually found out by friends. Do friends suffer in the same way as lovers from the glad, anxious, possessive drive to exchange histories? "You stop here, with me" – lovers scribble over and over one another's records until the two narratives pick up on the same leaf in a single, master hand.

No. You knew that. Friends have a curious, happy impatience. They have no urge to communicate everything-all-at-once; but, when they do have to refer to their separate pasts, the reference is made quickly. The reference is made *as if* to something they already hold in common. It is not a powerful, dangerous gift, but the endorsement of a valid currency. They feel as if they only need to be reminded of the details of one another. Unbrushed by jealousy, they may not even pay much attention to what is being divulged. They listen almost without interest, feeling no need to place themselves *as if* in the past of the other person. They do not feel displaced, as they do not wish to take over each detail as a signpost on the path that led inevitably to the loverlike consummation of You and Me. They are sure that, somehow or the other, they might as well have been there as not. Friends lose their terror of people vanishing, whereas lovers are encouraged to harp on death.

Time is abolished, in the present continuous of friendship. Space may ache a bit. Two friends meet after, say, three years in different countries. It is not as if they had seen each other yesterday. It is not as if they have seen each other all along – the mind's eye has its own rules, and does not do substitutions. They have, instead, a curious, happy sense of inevitability. They recognize one another less, but they know one another more. Who they see is who their friend *must have been*, all along. Memory does not disappoint itself by trying to make any of the images tally. Not losing sight of the past, including the past of the mind's eye alone, memory enriches the continuous present of friendship with a security of becoming. Risk is irrelevant, as is desire for risk.

You are monstrously idealistic. "A friend in need is a friend indeed." Are you scandalized to learn the common meaning of this: that needy people seek you out when there is something for them to get out of you. Hadn't you vaguely connected it to King Lear, taking it to mean that true friends are those who stick with you even when you are in need, and cannot afford to give them presents. "It is better to have loved and lost than never to have loved." This, too, you must have taken to mean: let us love, though we must part, it is sweet though tragic – the bargain struck with themselves, with varying degrees of realism, by young girls expecting to die of consumption, war brides, et cetera, before they make the commitment to the upheavals of lover/beloved. Did it never occur to you that this saying possibly deals only with one side of the emotional equation – that 'lost' means 'failed to win', the love remained unexpressed or unrequited, and what is 'better' is that the isolate lover is rewarded by having had a deeper experience and perhaps having acquired a more complex understanding of – I don't know what? Is there always a moral? Is some experience merely brutalizing, even self-cancelling through repetition, acquired at too much cost?

"I have to ask, whether this was before or after you exhibited the photograph which appears to be a yellow abstract, but is actually the egg of the Roc, smashed during incubation?"

"It was afterwards, when I saw how the veins were pumping on her wrist, how her wrist staggered as she agitated the colander, as if the fury of her outcries that Wednesday afternoon had not yet quitted possession of her mind . . . yes, it was then that I realized my fear."

The stranger did not pause. Nor did he flick his cuffs. I interrupted. Need I add, Jeremy, that the stranger and I were seated opposite one another in a railway carriage, dissatisfied customers both. The train had covered its distance from Doncaster, dragging a hundred minutes with it. Now it seemed disposed to clog up Birmingham New Street for another half-hour, as if needing to rest for a while, mulling over its ironclad disappointments. As I say, I interrupted the stranger in the course of his narration, to enquire:

"The colander?"

"Spinach tagliatelle," he answered, without hesitation. His tone was muted, but there was no change of pace. The shantung-jacketed stranger dipped his long melancholy face at a more acute angle to his rolled-up copy of the Financial Times, and delivered himself of the following:

February. The castle.
Dark stones. Sleek Norman scope.
    Inside the yard (once) prisoners who begged for food.
  It was a thoroughfare.
The castle's function was not action.

    Crocuses are coming up.

    Walk through razed walls, diagramming thunder,
consult the board. See where the stepped approach
once was formed? Swerve – blocked – The wellshaft filled?
Start falling.
    Stop. Visitors. Don't coincide.
Americans, boys, both climbing. Their parents
shine, twinned morning-after valentines.
Wait. They are gone.

    The city's length devises worlds.

    Take notice   of that hungry lapse when
you have wished someone away   and they
do leave. Significance not weighing
in that rush to void where they had been,
the emptiness attaches you, countervails thought.

    It is bright, but very cold.

    Here we persist, not waiting for a hint
from night   not waiting for a scene
of speech   or pain to warm: two future ghosts
whom stillness lifts.

Experience is coterminous with the words for it, which are also too slick for it. These initial words are never up to the excitement with which they produce themselves. The words are excited by the skill that goes into them, which is the unconscious skill of habit. They are excited by their own increasing, which seems to them like an increasing skill. This is what Monsters call an *emotion of the intellect*. There are emotions of the intellect. The emotions of the intellect require, but do not have, their own vocabulary. People tend to discuss them by analogy with the other emotions – the usual kind. These analogies behave as if they were no more than the truth. They behave as if they were quite as immediate as the words and the words' emotions. Great loss results from this. The body gloats. Metaphor seizes yet more unwarranted power. Monster experience is counted as actual only when Monsters re-experience the said experience in such a way that the words that go with it begin to dance and finally filter out. In this tranquillity the Monster is allowed to feel the shock of the shock, without words, not the nothingness of shock, after the nothingness of shock. Monsters do not discuss emotions of the intellect. This is taboo. It is embarrassing. Great penalties go with it, such as the loss of hair three to six months after the event.

TIREDNESS POEM

I

Hung up
on weather

Temperate sunset: something that never comes
because it goes too slowly

Tropical sunset: something that never comes
because it went too quickly

The stretched day holds the intermediate term
The held day stretches the indeterminate time

smooth to a fretted sootheness

sea to this
worn boulder

II

A short person
is exalted
by a parapet

The traffic the sea

"You are oppressing me with kindness,"
she said,
as if lightly;
"No, not at all,"
he said,
as if kindly

Jump, jump

III

Sea vistas
azaleas

What is too much for a month
and – is not – for the rest of the year?

Somebody else in the house
is busy

who makes wood creak
who makes wood pigeons drop their voices

I fought with her in my dreams last night,
the servant-thinness

the mushroom girl

IV

Maximum profit
does not account for, is not well served by,

the lacks and excesses
of – human nature? human needs?

seas and lands,

I am crushed between greenbacks –
Put pennies on my eyes

That man is making
maximum profit
of our conversation
in a dying condition

When do stalkers believe that they are lovers, and why do they sound the same? Decades in age and hours of time-zone and an infinite ladder of snobbery apart, these two men say:

"Hel-lo, You Know Who It Is. Heh-heh. So what are you doing, babe, I have butterflies, do you have butterflies? Why you never call me? I thought we were friends! I should turn up on your doorstep one of these days and see the expression on your face! I would like to see the expression on your face then! I should do that! I shall turn up on your doorstep and see what you do then! But why you never call me if we are friends!"

"Hel-lo, I've been in the area, and I've got your number, and I'd like to see you, if you'd like, but I have heard that you are difficult to catch – So – Maybe – I shall just – Drop – In, I'll drop in one of these days!"

I feel – I feel a song coming on!

1. (Do You Have My) Mobile Number – Hot Banana
2. Six Per Cent Love – Zero and the Long Division
3. Let Me Be a Balloon for Just One Day – Solitaire
4. One-Legged Sailor Boy – The Treasure Hunters
5. Yea Yea Nay Nay – Flocks at Night
6. Bread and Butter – The Oysters
7. Curved Time – Quarkety Quark
8. Sunshine Shelf – Fun Striped Kickboards
9. Zoid Zoid – The Voidettes
10. And Sir Galahad Wore Pink – King Arthur's Queens

I watch the host gladhanding the guests / and I'm lost / because the rest of the party for me is you / and you stand as blind as the / dial-tone/ of an / off-white telephone / I can't stand next to you / can't stand it / nothing to do but make an appreciation of a / pipe-dream situation / wired up to expect that in time you'll detect the / glitter on my cheeks is / out of a bottle and my / eyelash sweeps are conducted at / full throttle / if you're singing you / weep and I'd rather / speak / but my determination is / satin and your isolation is / metal

Silence Poem

I

Theseus

I think that our relation is theatrical.
You wear a crab-like, clay-like, or bedevilled mask,
And move within an oblong window, tragical,
Encased in tons of oolite, gazing. Streets cascade,
Each sun breaks caramel, the belling stone is young,
Is swift, compared to how your visor nods to see
Without quite looking. I know this, as if I'd gone
To sleep eight years on weaves, obliquely opposite
That quarry-featured building, in a hunter's hide
Among intransigents and transients. Who can wait
For signs of life so long, without a sign of life?
Whose power is more, the more you are expressionless?
This morning, at half five, the day was eau-de-nil,
Drowning the watching trees downwards from the crown.
By that light I shall set to work your fear in me,
To judge your stance, today to meet you, carnivore.

FAIR PHANTOM

Porcelain
     like innocence
          shames us.
The power to hurt and be glad –

translucence
like milk pearled through water
if milk did not dissolve in mist.

The matching set
bowl saucer egg-cup
         shine

brimming
     curved shallow
deep at last
seen six days a week twice at seven

when perfection has one revenge.

The days held upon us are convex,
nights
concave
as things tend to summer.

The year brightens out of forgetting,
aflame with itself   calibrated,
brings, to sit beside it, memories

alive in the capacity for symmetry
the appearance of a likeness
with what once was.

No   calendar   exactitude
Links   almost   dawn   with   afternoon.
Rest is relative,   is uncommon.
                    Needle pushes through cloth.

II

NARCISSUS

'No love without increase of loneliness.'
Your eyes are my eyes, and they frighten me,
As anything too underwater does.
They cannot be reflected perfectly.
Their circuit's live – they hold me held away –
Still wavering, that face – no chance to move
Towards precision, or from gorgeousness.
Youth has designs on age, projecting love,
But I practise erasure, watching this,
Encircling vanity with seriousness.
I break through warnings, like a cause of pain.
An asking silence rises from the pond.
My would-be lover overused my name –
Her silence drops against it, to rebound
Upon me, stone to sear a whitening rind.
The people calling – I've outlasted them,
I did not care to have them dreaming me.
Sun shoved. They made the leap from brink to rim.
Under water packed with mud, they lie
Between erosion and geology.

CONVIVIAL

No I do not want to sit
opposite you at lunch
(bunch together with some stranger
shouldering my shoulder?)
learning the show of 'Attentive!',
yet never collusive; glass-giving,
missing splice-shivered with meeting,
leaning like neutralised kissing,
conflicting mouthing swivelling
glistening into locked
looks. I like you too much to sit
opposite you at lunch –
much rather beside you inside
one same side of our overeyed edge,
lodged love eschewing pond-pleasure's
torrential self-selfed consequential
unleisurely ease made against
grained gaze, space gleaned between
fatiguing meals, crock-occupations.
Nonconfrontation? I like it
in public, with double-breath rhythm
near warmth, each the colourfall
spelling obliquely peach-presence
essential as background. Who's there.

III

ORPHEUS

Ghosts are at the head of human categories.
Unembarrassed, parasitical,
Without exertion they can make their wishes felt,
Their strength of changelessness exceeding will.

Dragging your feet in love to love, you followed me,
But changed. The shock of finding you was cold.
I looked back. That decided you. Serenity
Lay in regression. World to cave my world.
Often, striking, rapid, someone cuts across me,
Not showing human – one long shine of air –
Each time, that has been you; each time, not you. And I
Record your negative trajectory.
The working thought of you is like the stops of speech:
Memory, metre, power, grief, and health.
Having left you, I shall never have you lose me.
Inalterable silence, drop of hell.

NET

i believe in nothing
let me believe in time

i believe in nothing
that i may believe in time

nothing
except
time

IV

HADES

It was quite quite cold when you thought of talking,
Though hardly formal. Your spit froze at my feet.
Your stomach bitter, lungs drowning, bitterness,
Your mauve mouth staggering, your eyes stammering,
As women put to water-death drank volumes,
Bursting under sentence to destroy themselves.

Your bronze comb (my gift) nips its teeth in your scalp,
The span of your nape. – Take a pomegranate.
Don't speak of going back. We are silted up,
The mote, the jot, in a mothering earthquake's
Antique wrath.

– Your breath is a shaken-out shape!
Raging life, like a shooting star: luck falling –
You, leaving – My heart now bunching now splaying
Like a hunting-spider set running by hurt.
Except out of love, I do not answer you.

Come back to night. Exact, uncatchable differences in scale
Of things themselves, not just their ratio, emerge immensely,
Unprecedented night, every time the same, calyx of dodges.
Come in to night. I'm arbitrary as no god, seamlessly
Working you out in my silence. I cannot tell you how crazy
You are, your temporariness. I shall have taken you to wife.

THE MUD FLATS

Water that is
        indigo pressed together,
stain lines into cross-sectioned muscle

water that is arm
        that is snake inescapability,
loop that will not close

water that is
        finitude
no sound or sight of end or relevance to hope

this is what makes
        ships want to keel over
on land,
        whatever to avoid,
ships give up, self-abandoned
on voicings of
motioning sedge,
        motion that is
this way then that way
hisses: the constant
(guess from that swish the gulp and swallow
of water that seems unmoving unmoved)

water that is
where light is made to leave early,
before sun darts down
beneath the horizon
just beyond the black chapel
far left, off the path,
a house not to be walked to
a square set hollowed
for the drowned

These are the mud flats.

Wished to be remembered as specimen of dark:
not dark of passion or human deprivation –
nor dark of actualities (criminal dark) –
not insomniac, dayreturn dark:
Wished to be where blaze partakes of twilight,
where evening is explicit of,
a shimmering inversion of,
night before dark,
night before night,
night after night
dark after night.

The best poem would be a single word repeated. Cold cold cold cold cold. Monotone. Monotone.

The word is *intentionally opaque*. The search for
its meaning would scatter its sound.
Any deducible meaning amounts to a hint.
Not a key. Not a suggestion.
The word is *intentionally opaque, and also*
continuous with a purpose.

This is almost
an analysis
of his index
of   faint
jack
saint jack the faker
the anatomist he loves you to bits

Seduction: agreeing to be tempted.   solution isolation
Temptation: agreeing to be excused   consolation solace

Lux Æterna Et Perpetua

It is possible to haunt your own house. Being alone: one of the best times in the long process – not always visible to others – of being alone is when, late in the evening, I shut the door for what I know for certain is the last time that day. Then I turn to the house and I am smiling, for the house is alive with that live quietness which places have at night, especially places which are largely inhabited by a form of active emptiness, as this living-room is; hardly the dust whispers there, the main motion in it having been the practice of yoga sequences and basic tae kwon-do patterns, and the slow unfolding of a few purple irises in a tall vase against a green wall. Most of the village around me is asleep, or in transit elsewhere. The live quietness contained in my house and which night brings out is mine to be part of, to move through, to have in silence or to stir with speech declaimed as loud as anyone can or wants to make it. Poetry is spoken in the silence of the live house at night. I am on good terms with objects. They go at their own pace, and there is no guarantee – also no competition – which of us will outlast the others, inanimate or animate.

SHAPE OF A VASE

dealt in sharp colours
crowded in an alone room
lime green weed purple
bought on the highway
cat's eye thanks cat's purpose
salt and grease boxes
here's flowers for you
trimming into the trash can
stems drink deep for roots

If you like long, sharp shapes, it is possible to keep two bunches of purple irises in the green glass jar in the kitchen, and see them fail to open, and not be much dismayed, because there is the shape of their leaves. It is like an assertion, in the course of conversation, which turns every person into a listener, including the one who spoke. The light is sliced at the edge of their leaves and seems to part, falling away in outline. Brilliance precipitates out shadow, unlike rose leaves where the light softens across the surface, diffuse. Unopened irises. If you keep roses in the tall white vase in the living-room, against the green wall in the corner where there is least natural light, again this is for shape. The overhead lighting stamps a silhouette of the flowers onto the wall, stark and black and ungraspable. It is possible to be haunted by roses, which are over-rich and dim with significance, like ghosts. The silhouette of roses is never a haunting, but a definition of the essence of rose. It is as definite as the silence when you look instead of speaking, the silence drawn in to someone else's mind, drawn in by the breath between a smile that deregulates the exchange of greetings.

The grass had reached a dizzy pitch of green. It was rolled and English. Library buildings impended on three sides. The car park, on the fourth, closed what was almost a quadrangle. The narrow open road beyond the sparsely used car park was faced with more libraries.

She was sitting on the grass. They had just had lunch. Typically unclear on the telephone, he had invited her to lunch "at a place called the Butterfly. Do you know the Butterfly? I will take you there."

The Butterfly: it sounded like an oriental café. Would it be embarrassing to eat with a Chinese poet in front of Cambridge Chinese waiters? The embarrassment would be hers. First she would have to ask for a knife and fork. Then she would have to determine which dishes were ritually safe for her to eat, and which had sneaked in extracts of (dirty) pig or (sacred) cow. Taste would hardly influence her choice of dishes. Last, there would be the student power struggle of who would pay, how much, and how, complicated by maleness and femaleness. She did not even bother calculating the likelihood of truth in the story that women who had dessert were signalling their agreement to have sex. Difficulties were close enough at hand. They did not need anything so far-fetched. The Butterfly: she saw it complete. There would be pale-blue napkins folded like wings. They would slide from lap to floor. The specially ordered cutlery, which would turn out to be tiny fork and outsize spoon, would be stained with meat-like substances that reflected vaguely coral under the mercury vapour lighting. A real pink rosebud would jostle the aquarium-green plastic sprig of fern. The vase would be a modified cornet shape. The décor, gilt-edged white ceramic on microwaveable white ceramic.

Perhaps the Butterfly was not the Butterfly. It had been very unclear. The line from a pay phone in the bus station to a mobile phone in a shared house is unideal.

The Butterfly had not been the Butterfly. He had meant the Buttery, on the library compound itself. Like some other disappointments, this was a relief.

"Let me get this. What are you having?" His courtesy was peremptory.

She looked at the unfilled, refrigerated, open shelves. There was a scant selection of clear plastic and clingfilm, enclosing items that were priced and listed as food.

"One of these." She had to hesitate. His eyes were resting on the ticket beneath the salad. It cost more than a pound. "Maybe."

"I usually have one of *these*."

The inflection was that of a satisfied teacher. He grabbed a thickly frosted muffin. It looked like he was making a big exertion, as if he needed strength to pluck it from the tree whereon it grew. The gesture implied, Follow my example, now that I have made the effort.

"Oh, I think . . . so will I."

In the event, he did not remark on the waste, though pleased by her feminine lack of appetite. She managed half of the banoffee muffin before it succeeded in coating her teeth, preventing the need for further taste experiences, which is one way of downsizing appetite. Meanwhile, his cappuccino chocolate muffin disappeared. He gulped two styrofoam cups of tea, and spoke. She could not catch his drift, which was at once airy and acrimonious. No technique of summarization seemed to do justice to his speeches. She had to assume that she was missing something, something in translation, for he was rated as a good poet. Lunch was the time to speak of theories of poetry. Old equalled good. Difficult was better. Chinese poetry was matchless. English was unmusical.

She threw half her lunch in the bin. His eyes took notes. She wondered what he thought of her wantonness in disposing of the ruins of muffin. He habitually interposed reminders, in conversation, that many people in China are poor. He himself was far better electronically equipped than she, complete with computer system, video camera, mobile phone, whereas she had none of the above. He was twice her size, one and a half times his ideal weight. She did not know how to read this. The takings of many villages must have produced him, though why they had been fed into him, whether he had official connections or was the Chinese equivalent of a scholarship boy, she did not know how to begin to enquire. He watched her throwing away the food she had chosen, and let his face change. A full judgment had been made, a judgment that surely would be withheld.

After lunch, and the theories of poetry, it was time to talk personally. Now here they were, sitting on the grass. They moved their seat as the sun moved, because the cold still struck deep, in the middle of June.

He made his voice gentle. He told her that his spirit was gentle. Her own attitude ought to be more gentle: she was a poet too, and a teacher, she was a gentle person. A poet should have a heart of love for all the world. All the while, his hands snatched and tore at the manicured grass. The flesh of his hands was so plump that the nails seemed sunk in to it, not produced out of it. They moved so fast and so repetitively that she could not pay him single-minded attention. She kept waiting for some blue-suited university flunkey to come and tell them off. She would be guilty by association, by subordinate gender, and by exoticism of appearance. These foreigners might be educated, but they do not appreciate what's what.

There was no such interruption. No such person showed up. Nothing prevented the poet from continuing, as always, or is that as before.

It would take an effort to break through his artistic preoccupations. After all, his love for her no less than his love for poetry was the motive for this time spent together on the unseamed lawn. She could make the effort. If he was as crazy about her as he had said, it was right that he should know. As there was no chance for her to introduce the subject, she said what she had to say, in between what he was saying, but a little louder.

"I was once married. For a year. But I left. Now I am being divorced."

He stared at her, as if she really had thrown something important away. He stared at her as if she had broken something behind a glass case in a looking-only shop.

"Oh, you do not have to tell me this!" he cried with the voice he had used on stage at the Contemporary Poetry Conference.

He crumpled forward. She could cope with drama, but she was not willing to be dramatic. It was her cue to stare. He let himself fall sideways on to the grass, and reached for her hand.

"Tell me, tell me," he said, in a sobbing voice.

The cadence was perfect. She was disgusted. When had she desired perfection in anyone except herself (and her parents, and her brother, and her best friends)? She smiled, and said nothing. He evidently supposed that there was something of quite a particular kind that she ought to say in response. A recitative of night-wandering and loss, leading into an aria of love and pain: why was that beyond her. Marriage was a contract. She had informed him of her legal status. She was aware that she had limited reality in his imaginative life. Perhaps he would have the sense now to ask about her financial status, or the whereabouts of her husband.

He sprang up.

"Well! Now we are speaking *very very very* frankly," he said.

Frankness among friends had been a great theme of his, from the beginning. He paused, and looked up at her. She did not prompt him. His face hardened. He threw out his trump.

"I have a wife."

Still she said nothing. Again he looked for her reaction.

"Not here. In China," he said, in a tone that implied that the meaning of the word *wife* is contingent on geography, and may be expected to change over time zones.

Still she said nothing. She stood without moving. She was aware of having the expression that is described as having no expression. To herself, she seemed not to be seeing with her bodily eyes. She seemed not to hear with the physical sense of hearing. She felt her head open out until it contained the great roar and vanishing of the air in the world, and the tilt of the earth's turning. Treachery was a mind-expanding drug. Her head opened out further. It had not yet reached capacity. Now it was containing the outrageous depths of cold, motion, and energizing dark that are summed up in the one word, *space*. Internal laughter was flickering like hot light around this consciousness. She sensed his increasing dismay as she held herself in to herself. She was triumphant in her stillness. It was one of those times when it is not necessary to ask: What is there that is not known already?

He was dancing around her. He could not find a sign that would tell him how to be. He was no longer smug.

"I thought you knew! You must have known. Didn't you know? But you know that people in China marry early. You must have known! I gave you a hint."

Another look came her way. He wanted to see if she appreciated that he had given her a hint about these facts. She was content to continue looking blank while space settled for her. She did not mind, if he decided that she was thick as well as strange and potentially ungentle. It suited her barbarian status. She was feeling barbaric. Her enjoyment of her own silence was becoming fierce.

His dance staggered to a stop.

"You mean, you really did *not* know?"

"I really did not know."

Of course, they stayed talking for several hours after that. They exhibited some of the behaviours of people attending to the beginning of something. He made an effort to be charming. He pelted her with shredded grass, and sang. He made solemn eyes. He plucked the grass. He told her a parable with which he had grown up. Grass, if cropped short, grows better. His apparent violence (not that he used this ugly word) was a way of helping it (gently) along. Grass, devastated by fire, renews itself in the spring. She chose not to voice her main criticism of these verbal offerings, which was not that, in his philosophy, damage limitation is irrelevant. It was that their literary quality reminded her too much of the muffin: sweet, sticky, dense, and cheap.

She decided to walk home, taking the long way, alone, admiring her hand-me-down dress the colours of fire in the summer sun, comfortable in her new shoes, needing no words for her decision never to see him again, the ephemeral stranger.

TENSES

It is a present without a destiny.
It is a perfect memory spoiling for another voice.
It is taking in verse tragedies above a dish of strawberries,
tiger summer with pooled curtains drawn.
Mistake's creation,
it is certain loss again.

Happiness follows its own laws, no more than beginning,
it is kind with the lie of a finger plangently coming to rest,
striped aspects.
The pastoral beauty of experimental cattle.
Mistake's creation,
seen through mortality red with sun.

So easily misheard is a statement of intention,
in the best belief of its being a statement of the harsh past.
An end-stopped orchard's fruiting.
The scooped chest's tendrils both soft and bitter.
Mistake's creation,
musician's duress in a listening test.

Things that are most themselves resemble one another. Heat and light. What is it that the mind's eye sees when you think in sentences? Would you credit a literal account? Don't you see sentences in your mind's eye, from time to time? They are in black, conservative-looking, in a small Times New Roman or perhaps Perpetua font; or they are carefully handwritten, with a nib fine and black as a corner eyelash, spaced to look like print. They are not inscribed on paper. They appear on a sand or gold background that shines softly without a sheen, porous, lightly flecked with the suggestion of a burnish or copper mottling. This background passes on and on to the left, which you experience as a screening backwards. Your mind's eye reaches forward, to the right. The refusal to pursue the words is one of the ways in which your mind tells you that it is tired. In a world without fatigue or mortality, what would prevent you from looking at the words, reading to know them and to rearrange them, watching them come towards you backwards from the right? The words are formed left to right; their background pushes in from right to left. The words are lit from above. Your ground is filled across, lit from behind. You see it is like skin. Hence your dislike of reading aloud. The skin of your mind's eye has unutterable voices.

DEEP COLOURS BLEED

the borders nailwhite.
inside the map
is solid terrain
in featureless black.
familiar wordgroups
presenting with failure
in the face of that.
that pontefract.

MONSTER CONSCIOUSNESS

Without reality, outside reality, beside reality (refrain). Modern city –
mediæval street plan – the refrain stringing a bead on a single
string, *monster consciousness*, the road's wide frame. Headed off by
the hungry swinging of skeletal cranes, all mechanical movements
and prehistoric frames. Detachable spires, each an enlightenment
to itself. When you have escaped from the place of concentration,
monster consciousness will make each subsequent place undergo
repeated intensifications, dazzling beneath the monster daze.
Monster consciousness calls down the abolition of unreality upon the
space framed by the gaze. Everywhere on the instant demands a
reckoning, side by side with everywhere else. Things get to the
Monster, things lodge in the Monster, things stop the Monster.
There is the experience, turning to memory, of pain. The Monster
has learned to compare this to a sharp object wedged in the flesh;
but the Monster is not so much at the mercy of new objects. The
Monster was born full of cutting implements that move around
within its own flesh, the wrong inside, keen and heavy. Monster
flesh enfolds these sharp objects, doing its best to soften them,
making terms with them under cover of living. Subject to recur-
rent fever, to running infections, *monster consciousness* has
fleshwrapped difficult things, deep, almost immobile, indistin-
guishable under the scanner, only moving again slightly and
seldom. *Monster consciousness* makes you cringe with its boundless
appetite for displays of health. It croons over insults. It likes appre-
ciation. *Refrain.*

IN THE LOFT

Since when the essence of cathedrals
is their emptiness of worshippers
but for the dwindled pilgrims to the sublime

The end of the day can have a scattering effect
spins out, spins away the chances for speech

To continue here I am an exile
to return home a traveller
expected to tell stories
in both places of settlement

The pity I feel for those who love openly
is archaic, and deserves the name of ruth

The bones of my face ache, as if,
season in, season out, I am gripped
by one of winter's illnesses

For the first time, I found the action of the
wind on falling leaves mildly depressing – a
chill about what might be termed my heart-strings.
It is 22 November, and still behaving like autumn.
The longer I live here, the more I notice
of the particularities of the year – the more used
I am to it, the more new it is to me, almost
terrible and striking in its quality of strangeness.
My eyes have become gradually more solitary,
accustomed to less future in which to look out *with*.

Othello's problem: difficult to believe, nearly impossible
to trust, so, correspondingly, the desire to give and find
all – where interaction is always barely recovered
from nothing, an unexpected something becomes invested
with the value he would place on all. To have excellent
defences is to be wholly vulnerable in any situation
that has an air of being ultimate.

I should be suspicious of anything that seems sudden.
It is a thing probably quite everyday, yet before
this thing, I trip over a formation lying in wait
within myself.

In love again, you are asking?
– No.

With him, you must have been – ?
Yes I was, yes at first, largely through misinterpretation
and the desire to love. And all my friends
were relinquishing their independence, one by one,
around me.

But when he, didn't he – ?
Not much, not seriously. More what I would call
bullying than battering.

Why did you, didn't you – ?

I had to see that it was not an inadequate
expression of his desperation, mysteriously provoked
by a mysterious inadequacy in me. It was
adequate to itself, as an act of power.

Is reconciliation ever adequate to what has gone before?

To express modesty is already a skill.

The difference between "I shall have been," as an
assertion, and "Am I?"

The breathtaking corpse on the stage implies the
repeatability of tragedy, even while the evocation
of death asserts its uniqueness.

In tragedy, the fears of the audience are confirmed.
This means their optimism may be untouched. In
love, we feel that our love is unique, and at
the same time, feel that we are part of the community of
lovers who love the same way: comedy plays
to our hopes. In dying, we die alone our particular
deaths, but death is the same and our bodies
are interchangeable. Comedy and tragedy, in
sequence, will find tragedy to be of the greater
weight – fear confirmed not hope applauded. I
was myself. Someone may have been.

With whom would I have been more than myself
most myself I would

Monsters do not remember how to talk to people who allow the Monsters to love them. There are whole tones of voice and expressions of snout that they have lost. If they tried to mouth their love now, it would hiss and bray like discourtesy and fear. It is not that they have no conception of dulcet tones. They low and howl in minor keys, their head a little on one side, looking at the new moon through glass, their living room a city of spilled salt and their apartments permanently rigged with walked-under scaffolding. Then they wait in hope for a like response from humankind. They retire to the floor to undertake their feeding, in a room where the curtains are drawn against the light of day and the scent of white lilac. Monsters live in an atmosphere of burning: burning essential oils; burnt toast. It is the closest that these sweet-natured beasts can get to living out an infernal identity – this smell of burning. This hellish approximation is another way that Monsters seek to please, or oblige, the world.

If you wish to court another Monster, or to discover whether *Monster Self* lives beneath the integument of natural-fibre humanity that some acquaintance of yours presents as their social limits, a gift of food is a good way to begin. Present it in a little basket, decked with pastel ribbons. Monsters are ever so sweet and soft inside, because they are the painful embodiment of the dimensions of cliché when cliché happens to be true, when it is truer than true-to-life. These combinations are suitable for eating on the floor, without the aid of cutlery that bewilders monster paws scurrying to shovel up husks: Olives and ice cream. Pistachios and teething rusks. Little cereal squares, dried apricots, chocolate digestive biscuits, and individual tiny cheeses released from their orange plastic netting. Salad leaves, but nothing too wormy or too wet. Any bland items, such as paper tissues, rice paper, cupcake papers, used chewing gum (spearmint flavour), cocktail sticks, toothpicks, ice lolly stems, et cetera, are liable to be munched ruminatively, then spat out again like owl pellets. Unlike owl pellets, they never make it to the processes of physical digestion. Monsters permanently suffer from aches and gnawing in their unsatisfied jaws, something between teething and neuralgia. Unlike the sufferers from teething or neuralgia, Monsters do not become tetchy. Their chewing of bureau handles, balsa wood models, and window frames, is purely ruminative. Even the Monsters who eat black mud are doing no more than than living up to the Monster nature. They do not commit gross acts of rebellion against purity and nourishment. No, their habits are rather expressive of the gentle and self-absorbed Monsterdom, that chews over and over but will not consume. There is an undersea quality to Monster feeding. It is cleanly, it is not predatory. A Monster hoovering up the sediment is a sight to warm the heart. It is a myth, that they poison human beings with one look, one breath, one touch.

The friends of Monsters, if not themselves Monsters, tend to experience a degree of happiness that is not necessarily in proportion to their aptitude for happiness. In part, this arises from contrast. Monsters are witnesses to the happy population. Monsters are to-the-side-of-it, they are not-there-yet, they are to be addressed as if they bear, by rights, an unconscious, impersonal relation to your own happiness, which thereby affirms you in your place among the happy, who are few but who manage to outnumber Monsters. Monsters are never-to-be-there. They are the horizon, by which you understand the white-winged picturesque sunniness of your sailing ships.

If you succeed in befriending another Monster, it will pick you up and carry you when you are tired, or when you do not want it but the Monster thinks you want or need it, or when you want it for no reason, or when the going is rough in Monster terms. This may be disconcerting if it is a speedy variety of Monster. The speedier the Monster, the sharper it brakes. In fact, gradual Monsters are to be viewed with more trepidation. They croon to themselves and have a side-to-side gait (a generalization, but not altogether unfair), and may pitch you quite off their shoulder unless (a) you tell them a story to stop them crooning (b) you are yourself a speedier variety of Monster. The story must feature the performance of heroics by a thinly disguised version of the carrying gradual Monster itself. This will make it interrupt, to mend the narrative, usually though not invariably in its own disfavour. At any of these narrative intrusions, you may smack it behind the ears as if by mistake, and let yourself down unobtrusively while the gradual Monster is crying out to enquire if *you* are all right, since *it* is in pain.

All Monsters manage to be Parents. Few Parents succeed in being Monsters.

Monsters are not good at taking care of themselves as a matter of routine. No Monster thinks of itself as lonely. Monsters are frequently terribly pleased with themselves, to a degree that can be annoying, even when the non-Monstrous discover the insufficiency of the reasons or motives for this glowing Monstrosity of self-congratulation. If a Monster makes hot food for itself *and* eats it – herbed lamb chops with tea for an early breakfast, say – it feels comforted and tearful. It is irrationally certain that Somebody Loves It, as if it were young, fretful, and a little ill, in the den of its Monster Folk once more. Monsters are not so given up to pleasures of the senses that the physical sensation of being warmed from the inside and nourished may account for their sentimental happiness before hot food. The emotional memory of a Monster is stronger than its logic, and, looking after themselves, they are fooled into feeling that there is Somebody Looking Out For Them. Of course, this is never the case. Anyone looking out for them soon forgets to do so, becoming caught up instead in alternately looking at them and looking away from them, according to the Monster aspects alternately present to view. Monsters suffer from cold fingers, tense shoulders, blocked chi. Their temperature and pulse escalate and drop abruptly, with little relation to any but internal weather. Monsters are past masters at *somatization of symptoms* You would not wish to see a Monster faint. Even school-age Monsters have been known to faint, from an overdose of storytelling. In their unconsciousness, they dream and flail, sometimes with their feet in buckets or their heads against a wall.

Sarcasm and snobbery take a long long time to be effective as weapons against the *Monster consciousness*. If you look and look at a Monster, fixing it with your gaze and without trying to engage it in speech, it will not be embarrassed. It may even feel itself liked. Monsters are themselves on the lookout for the quality of silence. They take silence in others to be a sign of exercised choice. If you give a Monster the silent treatment, it will respect you for your ability to recognize choices. Monsters believe profoundly that the world goes according to patterns, large-scale and small-scale but detectable patterns, and they will refuse to view silence as a lapse or lack. They will look behind your eyes. If you try to disappear, they will be so overcome with admiration that the chase will be on.

Monsters are lyrical. They are not lyrical by conviction, but because they are driven to become so. They are the development of an *I* that is the expression of a vision. Their way of doing nothing means that they have no leisure time. Monsters are bedazzled momently. They are careful giants building a mosaic out of the generalities and particularities that assail them in the nature of perpetual observations. This mosaic is the index to *Monster sanity*. As the

Monsters sit building it, you notice their shadows, which are invariably in the shape of dogs worrying at a bone half-buried in cruelly heated and reflective sand. Some Monsters cast the shadow of terriers, on a ratty and kittenish tin and chicken diet. The ones to watch out for are the Great Danes, with half a side of elk, a quarter of Neolithic man, or an ostrich stuffed with diamonds landing up against the ragged rocks of their circling teeth. They whistle between their teeth as they build, and their shadows worry. It sounds like sedges.

A DAY OUTSIDE

I had not realised waterways
               Water was a forgotten way
          One moment glimpsed into another
there were more and more willows
                    pike
along the river bank
one
               One moment glimpsed into another
               round imperceptible metres
               making no waves
               glimpsed
(No idea what it is like to be working on the river nowadays)
        One to work the locks
        to walk the lock gates outwards
        pushing with the legs (Monks dug this canal)
               level
One to hold the craft still by moving forwards
to hold it still by moving back
. . .
Waterways I did not know I did not know . . . I
        exposed yet disappearing
        as a pillar of salt
        set to steer boats
               possible
The nonappearing summer rain

So these mornings, to wake from a nightmare to the day's tasks finds the only difference between the two states is in the variety of implausibilities.

Monsters have a beaten place inside them. Not 'beaten' as in 'defeated'. Beaten: lacerated, trembling, unbelieving, angry, proud, humiliated. Unable to move out of its own rawness, like a sore or like a song, it weeps. The ordinary air can be a real unkindness to Monsters. Ascertain their condition, before you invite them out for walks, unless you have a rarefied air for them, a walled garden with white flowers, perhaps. Their flesh is covered with scales but the air can strip it, exposing that which was meant to work unseen, the Monster innards half-healing, half-dying.

It is dangerous to consort with Monsters. Consider your own motives. Are you, by nature, a Monster hunter? Attracted by the seeming power and completeness of the Monster, the natural predator of the Monster will be driven by a resentful wish for mastery. The natural predator of the Monster will seek, first of all, its capacity for happiness, which is, need it be specified, Monstrous. Once the Monster's passion for companionship is discovered, you have discovered a strength which can be made into a weakness. Finally able to condescend to a vulnerability in the great Monster, the true hunter will use himself (herself) as the means of punishment: reasonless absences, chary presence, all will play upon the Monster's sense of its own beaten place. The true hunter will then feel able to give the Monster lessons in strength. This strategy tends to fail when the predator backs off, in fear of unleashing Monster furies. Then the Monster will pursue him (pursue her) frightfully, stupidly envisioning, through its retreating opponent, a chance for Monster and hunter alike which the Monster must encourage the hunter to make good. This has to be one of the oldest games in the book. Sooner or later the Monster gives up, often in the vicinity of a forest pool or deserted, enchanted fountain. Then the woods ring to the strains of yet another Monster torch song, the verses of *Greensleeves*.

Alas, my love, you do me wrong, To cast me off discourteously When I have lovèd you so long, And joyèd in your company . . .

THE RELIGION OF LOVE

I

I':   You'll get over it.

I":   Oh, do you think so?

I':   Don't you?

I":   Oh, do you think so? For the last X years it has only changed to become more itself. When I could not avoid you, I tried not to look at you. When I had to look at you, I often tried to insult you. Eventually, I even sought you out, sometimes, and saw myself doing this. You were the negative reason to add to many choices I actually made as if for themselves alone, never for themselves alone. I would not become a creature of your mind. Without even being a creature of your mind, year after year day in day out I live in consciousness of you. Not that you are that important, not that you could be my obsession. You are simply that which is. The friends who envy or praise my freedom, my independence, my facility for happiness while living by myself, have no conception that even in my moments of most isolation my thinking has a trace of the ultimate thought – of you – I hide in you from you.

I":   Just be yourself.

II

Waiting to be punished for having shown affection (farless desire,
let alone desire) is something that they have learned so well to do.
Their second nature has a hanging head.

True and transparent happiness is a moment not to be reckoned
with. It follows such years of secrecy in which the heart condemns
itself. Tâche d'être heureuse? Rather be silent. It would be a release
from effort, to acknowledge the movement towards happiness
which is more than they can bear to admit.

The difficulty is selection. I find it hard not to remember things.
Except for the years when I forget entire people and whole swathes
of time, I remember pathologically. And in the years when they
were forgetting, forgetting themselves, they remembered – remem-
bered, especially, you. And you. And you. Their constants, their
invisibles, not knowingly mine. To have someone to remember
when I was forgetting myself . . . It seems like a self-cancelling
luxury . . .

III

They find an eroticism in parallels that never meet except, as they tell us and we are taught to look forward to, at infinity.*

* Monsters never learn.

MONSTER HUNTING

It must be remembered that Monsters only seem to smile at you with animal innocence. In fact, they believe themselves to be more advanced beings, although they are natural prey. It is not through a lack of appreciation for home comforts or the decorative arts that Monsters prefer blank walls or open spaces. It is because these blanks, to Monster vision, at any moment are expected to blink and peel, to start coming away in unexpected shapes, of script or Monster images. Monster atmosphere is permanently disturbed, and sensitive predators would find this disturbing. Their space is a procession of significant presences. Hunted or not, the Monster is solitary without being lonely. The Monster is the bizarre, derivative heir of the human storybook explorer, sitting at his fire in his semi-artificial clearing while all around him the eyed jungle gets on with its largely ignorable night. At any time of day, the Monster spiritually, or imaginatively, can be precipitated into this friendly clearing and indifferent night. Remember that, in the Monster's system of reckoning, *Monster* is the opposite of *Animal*, *human* being no more than a subset shared by both. Where the human has a sense of disjunction from reality, the real Monster relation to language is an enduring simultaneity of experience and implication, memory and expression. The innocence of Monsters is that they are born old.

Choose your camouflage, if you are a Monster hunter. You can involve the Monster in your movements. This method has been preferred by male hunters, but the modern Monster hunter is encouraged to diversify. In this case, note that your sensitivity and your vanity can look identical, and can draw the Monster in towards you, until it is too late for the Monster to adjust to the way that you judge it. If, on the other hand, you take an arrogant attitude towards the Monster that is your intended prey, note that the Monster is better able than you to differentiate between vanity and power, even if you are a female hunter who tends to camouflage power as vanity when hunting either sex of your own kind.

REMOVE PACKAGING BEFORE USE

There's something unsatisfactory about my chatter,
like an object that falls unpredictably further
(in unstable equilibrium);
I weight things wrongly, like the giant who got up after eating
    moderately for hours:
beneath his chair, the floor was powder.

All this by way of prologue.

From a college lawn I gathered a goose feather
to remember a friend by; he was asking me whether
(though I'd done History of the Language)
I knew 'gospel' meant 'good news', and wouldn't it be better
to have a personal god as my saviour?

The Sole Creator: 's he a maniac stranger
like the one who sent my friend a declaration
(under cover to her supervisor) –
in every word each letter pencilled in a different colour
by the would-be lover?

Pattern and diversity prove nothing.
There was the friend who found that she enjoyed teaching
(contrary to her expectations) –
as a schoolgirl, she'd once had to decorate five hundred muffins,
she liked it after the thirty-fifth icing.

LETTER FROM A MONSTER TO A MONSTER IN SCOTLAND

Dear Monster, Schatzi,

You say you have no voices in your head anymore. How do you know what to do with yourself. You cannot think that you are hungry. You cannot even think, there is some hunger. Before it is thought, the hunger ties itself into a navel of discontent. It flips upon itself and vanishes. There is no use dropping cyanide-rich appleseeds into an unlit convexity. Monster, you do not want to think the sky is blue. It turns towards you a split-level welkin with blundering clouds. It is no more or less than atmosphere, degraded, without rim or guarantee, menacing because ineffable. You do not speak, Monster, you skip stones like words across water into which they fall and sink, hardly having skimmed, and my word is good for nothing, because it exists only in hope of a future, and the light of the future you read by, Monster, is as without promise as it is without a plausible past.

Does death still not interest you, Monster. That lack of interest is not why I have died. You have to have each moment like a whole life in a wide band of lives, all the time in the world every day, the plaining planning chattering sparking wailing soothing begrudging whispering glorying voices in your aeroplane-view head. Do you notice, Monster, do you communicate, do you have an end in sight or an end in mind?

Monster, I know you are wondering, so I shall tell you. I am in an inherited house whose furnishings dematerialized during my sleeping carelessly, and now I sleep watchfully. I am writing to you in between a few little sleeps, but the wakings are indifferent, the same. You know, and I know, Monster, that this is not a privileged position. Does the apex of your roof bore down upon you, so that you are paralyzed inside a pyramid concentration of no-matter-always-later-on.

I would begin from scratch, but I am a beast with claws and antlers, so that I do not know where to begin. There is nothing against which to rub off the velvet from my branching skull. My claws shredded the specimen plantings. Hybrid beasts have no proper function, so it useless to coax them to perform. Nobody trusts me with their begonias, let alone their bamboo furniture.

Monster, do you miss somebody so much, without knowing who it is, that it does in place of the hunger that refused a name. Monster, if you were more simple, you could decide to recognize a stranger. You could jump to the conclusion that that person, or that other person, was the stranger who sculptured an absence within you. You could pretend to have an absence within you, and then you could claim that the absence was a loss. You would greet a stranger as if he embodied a conjunction. You would see him as the One whom you lost when you failed to find each other. You could deny love and hate, and swear that all you want is recognition, of your other, better self. You would be content to pass on, having achieved this recognition, as if you had passed a test, as if you had crossed a border. Monster, you have lyrical tendencies. No, I am not accusing you of anything.

As I write to you, Monster, the field is tipped with pink. There are two unconcerned horses, facing different ways. To my left, there is a hill scythed parabolically, an angular miniature fortification grey at the top. Why do Monsters make the landscape passive.

There were two horses unconcerned with each other, each alive with horse-concerns.

Moving south, I am trying to think of you in the north. When I think of you, I can see in my mind's eye only coastline, slate waves, rust shore, and egg-white sky. So many nights in the past, Monster, we thought that you were nearly off to drown yourself, and now you are painting yourself right up against the flood.

Remember that question that invents its own, untenable premise: why do women write more letters than they post? Monsters surpass such transactions. Such speculations are none of ours. Monster letters are sent without being received, received without being sent. The two kinds balance out, in a series of flurries, near misses, and *snarling*. Aaah.

WHAT IS YOUR GUY REALLY LIKE?

Mr. Performance is not too happy.
Another survey has been done on him.
He saw it onscreen in his wife's study,
Before she quickly clicked and minimized.
He glimpsed it obliquely in the mirror
She keeps next to her. During long downloads
She plucks her eyebrows and attacks her hair.
Her mystery is that she seems to have none.
She also does not hide the pot of wax
Destined for stripping from her burning legs.
But she hid the survey. He saw her click.
He is even more hurt than by her friends.

Mr. Performance is distracted.
He eats a pot of chocolate elbow cream.
Mr. Performance denies he bought
Venison sausages, or organic
Hot dog rolls; Mr. P. denies he thought
Of doing a course in Thai massage; Mist'
Perf. denies liking real country music;
Mr. Performance is taken aback
(Not to say sexually challenged) by his
Own name. Doubts his existence. Poor record
With ice cube trays. He called his wife VENUS.
Now she has transformed him into a quiz.

Does the answer really lie in fleece blankets?
This was the tragedy of Mr. Performance. Oh, man.

Dry Clean Only

Happiness comes off them like powder from a moth's wing, I
stand, looking in dismay at my smeared hand,
uncomprehending, while the winged settlers change
their alignment, their languages of shift in
relation to light, I stand, looking at the
evidence, a little life used up, the velour of
movement, cold running water is a need.

Night. Almost always, **night indoors**. Darkness is a substance, a stuff which, like the stuffs learned about in classroom science, you regularly apprehend, but have no tools to comprehend it. The fear of sitting up in the dark, sticking your head into that stuff, exposing the already vulnerable upper body to the swings and whims of whatever moves the darkness of the **night indoors**. For it has a rhythm. The curtain-long shadow at the doorway – curtainless and doorless – to the alcove opposite the bed: that pulses, and seems without source. The sequins and starfalls behind your lids write themselves on the **night** when you open your eyes. Their colours are of an undersea intensity. They sink and rise, discrete entities, they sank and rose, as if along the heatshafts of volcanic water or beneath cold currents well below Atlantic waves. Sound is both hushed and magnified, resembling – beyond any communication – something intent.

You would sleep slowly, if you slept. Sleep without dreaming, dreaming without sleep, dreaming without dreaming. The bed would rock free of its moorings. The floor is no longer to be counted on. The rhythm's whims and swings would take you as their own. A bat might drop a guava on the galvanized metal roof; the fruit would roll along the guttering, then drop straight down to a pulping, the sound of its impact absorbed into the house wall. A cat might walk on the roof, treading like a Scandinavian ghost. The cherry tree on the east side, the guava tree on the north – the white lilac tree on the east side, the neighbour's dogwood on the north – would scrape their branches on the house or on the fence, on the wall or on each other, articulating an indifferent patience to and of the wind: that is the sound of their growing power. They are slower even than your sleep, than your dreams.

Monster Vision

Night persists for a longer time in Monster brains than tallies with the actual measure of daylight, or Monster adaptability to the halogen environments in which Monsters must survive. Monsters are very bad artists. They hoist their bulk with a grand air of procession, so the observer credits them with a certain acuity of vision. In fact, they see little except by guesswork. Their brain chemicals, the slippage of time zones, and the availability of artificial light have done for Monster vision. The Monster looks at you, and you feel seen through. The Monster sees you with a purple halo and a golden aura, against a backdrop populated with troubled shapes in two dimensions, yellow black blue gold. Monsters have their vision, but they have half lost their sight.

King Vertigo and Queen Momentum

King Vertigo

I

He never said just that:

'This is my gift. I,
for once in our lives,
show us non-change, hold
out, feel? deliver
thing from thing.

'End hurtles to end,
needs driving meeting.
Flash of metal and
slash of forgetting
makes us home.

'Alternative cures
contain contentment,
get us going, quick
jabs of old slowness,
a pure booze of breeze.

'I am telling us
what it is like the
second time round, and
again, and again,
and again.

'Stone into flesh into hair into hair into flesh into stone.'

INSECURITY MEASURES

He never said just that:

'It's night, again, behind the fine cabinet,
and in male barking regrouping the spiked street.
Night again. I can believe I was a child.
Indoors, it is fine with you.
        Child with twig swirls
powerful in snail-wet setting concrete, limns
anglo-saxon ribbon entrails interlaced
with chinese kite-tails, rife chromosomal knots.
For years that surface tents a remembrance dance.
        Foil-haired child,
too many decades on. Swirl
till convergence. Compare to london english
final sounds: death, deaf.
        Admired vandalising,
am I real, more frequent than banality
in your eyes?
        No-one can help, no telling me,
who will impress, refilling wine, sleep smiling.
Score unhelp into other people's driveways.
Nobody stops, or says to stop.
        I need both.
That red-soled footgravure was a ballad shoe.'

III

WISDOM IN CHARACTER

He never said just that:

'I am a monster for forgiveness.
Promises: are made to be broken,
lovers: devoured like a tonic.
Friends to be offended – guests wounded –
specifications to be thwarted –
luck denigrated – ritual hurt –
humour frustrated – messages wiped –
repose tormented – meetings revoked.

How else can I take you up on what really matters?
Look at me, forgive me, I am way beyond too much!

Keep vigil with me at images.
Flicker and murmur in weariness
but do not forego the night. Archives
bow themselves beneath my blooded living-room.
My stained armchair splays prodigiously
atop a ritual fountain-jet.
I command you: disdain the giants.
Come, follow me, I'm not selling out.

The misery of telling something no-one will hear!
I've made demonstrations, lovably. Hold me in awe.'

IV

GONE TO PIECES

He never said just that:

'There are several quieter forms of happiness
than I would ever permit in my company
except when you and I, my sweet, have escaped.
Then fennel liquorices batwords tarring shut
before they jump your throat gorge inwards, vampirise
you, doom rising from your female nature's thwart.
Re-enter clarity with me, alma mía,
lie there, you will not have to begin on belief,
reclining, detail faith, moonstone corneas.
Your romance is with the deathriver's ferryman.
Yours is the only soul so hammocked back and forth,
relaxed like dumbness reading off my downturned face.

There is music, you are best to listen for it.

Internal sluicings and pressures,
beadswishing of blood's blueness,
your lyric timelessly ticking,
never to be snapped red by air.
The first, cast long and slow, movement
of the crunchbone sonata –
wild virtuosi record it –
plaining in your uptight back.'

V

King Vertigo

He never said just that:

'The efficient power of words over things:
Does it carry conviction straight into the mind?
The way that darkness carries cold
The way that famine carries plague
The way that skyline shoulders night
The way that nations prevail over maps
The way that earthquake carries graves
The way that stillness shoulders sound
The way that your retina bears my print
The way that my neediness battens on your heart.
Don't you feel that the world is lordless yet lawbound?
Don't speak of misfortune, it can be provoked –
What must happen might happen, and worse.
Don't you see that I am your magician for these times?
Seal the jar with a layer of oil,
The paste will keep forever. You I have sealed
Like a portrait in oils, staving off
The normal dawn, the preening of blinds,
The wrapping of work, the distraction of friends.
Haven't I saved you for black, pink, and gold?
Tarnishing brass is not more subtle,
A rabbit's paw is not so tender,
An executed promise is not as rare,
Rosa centifolia, lily of undernourishment,
Than the interest passing from your face into my paint,
No less than unrivalled, no less than I say.
Nothing you could think of would do against me,
Nothing you could manage would do against me!'

Queen Momentum

I

SUMMONING UP THE SPIRIT

Well my dear, I dreamt of you last night
in a preposterous turquoise dress,
a perfectly quiet swan cradled
under each of your arms, you dancing
in the corner of an empty room
like a music room at school, plastic
orange chair, fluorescent tube lighting,
your face concentrated, unsmiling
as a frightening angel from a
true religion, or a narrator
in a beautiful, difficult play,
you crowned with little candles, silence
dancing.

Alice and Leda and Elektra!
Top of the class, you outshone them all.
Where had they gone? Why was I standing
alone at the back, trying not to
catch your eye?
Why did I think the scrawl
on the blackboard was ancient Greek (a
language not taught in girls' schools, where I
come from)? Why no noises from chapel
or court? Why seem eternal as death,
not infinite as life, dancing? How
could I be sure that, if I opened
the door, the sky would white out, outside
nothing?

II

FELLING TREES

You summoned me, master,
you performed an operation on me.
On all fours up the drumskin stairs I fled
towards you, away from where
I no longer should be.

Your arms open, pointing.
There are two of them, hacking the great tree.
Gathers and clusters crash, yawing, dropping,
the profile increasingly defeated.
Smell: haemorrhaging green.

It is not limbs falling.
Each loss dips and welters, a perfect tree.
A name in repeated diminution,
syllable by syllable, less each time,
trashing identity.

The first sign was stormlike,
an ashy spasm of future hit the leaves.
Too localised, one thing alone shaken,
not by weather, by a human meaning,
successful surgery.

Roped up and conquering,
two sawing men are taking to the heights.
How gentle they are, agile, new-coloured,
gaining a foothold on zilch. They lower
the sky, the view of sky.

Sun hazes it, poison.
Tree falls, *inconvenience*, on garden ground –
the only horror the house will notice.
This is the world to bring children into,
master, just as we found.

III

DOPPELGÄNGER

There was, above us, that eardrumming pressure
of extension of water – I am
surrounded – extension of water to depth,
sight readjusted to a sun that flexes
through ice-pack turquoise, immersion in
the feeling of sound transposed too deep for reach,
which I'd first known in the grounds of a
plantation house turned country club – a festive,
desolate place, where a child had died
sliding in the playground (now abandoned, not
dismantled), near the front of the drive,
under (much, much older than anything else)
thick-timbered, moss-rigged trees – I had known it there,
in the back, where the disused fountain
could be supplied again if we stopped a duct
in the side of the open-air pool,
in exchange for a visible reflux of
filth from the ages of its basin.
The remains of an avenue confounded
temperate ideas of the seasons,
green boughs shedding rust, fawn, ochre leaves, setting
them floating with us, unregarded
as potential symbols of renewal and
decay. – The ladder down the deep end.
Water: pressure: depth: sound: light: intertextured,
I knew there first, an adventure of
dismay.
            Not in that place, but in that medium,
I dreamed her. It was our first meeting
for weeks. She lay on her front with apparent
ease, with a young face and a backward
stream of luminous hair, legs bent up to hold

her feet, yes, just like a mermaid's tail,
while she chuckled with her old inscrutable
delight. 'You see, you thought I had changed:
well, I haven't.' I was pleased, and, trying to settle
into conversation at long last,
smiled a little frantically, near bursting,
wondering how she had managed it,
knowing how soon I would need to break things off,
perhaps before we were properly
talking, I already felt the pressure to
start to the surface and breathe. Would I
find her again? About to excuse myself,
I looked towards her. Silver bubbles
were rising from the side of her canny smile.
She was comfortable, waiting.
                                        I
had to surface quickly, it was urgent,
I had to, from her, from water, from
sleep.

IV

LILIES

The room heaves with scent before you see them.
A humming smell, thicker than polished church.
Vaginal cyprine. Gelled and sweetened ashes.
Between your fissured teeth, a crush of cloves.

A pallor which does not go through phases.
Extravagance is all, couture white,
A claw-shape of undersea dictation.
Albino buds unclose crustaceous birth.

Haunting, hunted. Exquisite. They require
Another lexicon than I possess.
A toxic bouquet of hitchcock-women
Compelled to a longstemmed waterglass death.

You tell me their pollen stains are serious.
A different tropical from what I know –
A burning continent – they look glorious.
I cannot gauge their habits by my own.

They will stand: lovely, oppressive, alien
To my traditions as your cult of Eve,
Brought to my house as a gift from someone,
To be arranged in absence of belief.

V

FLESHED PERSPECTIVE

Tourism is inadvisable among these rocks.
The tutelary spirit is a giantess,
so uncompromising, she has no space for eyes,
but frowns with her mouth, and even prefers
a drink of pure fear to a draught of death.
Her outline greens into view from over the top.
People have been known to lose their heads here
in respect of emptiness. Their blood leaps and knocks.

"Intreat me not to leave thee,"

And then I woke up with a skinful of ratfur
on a causeway where broken bottles constellate
and I did the dance yet again in crêpe-paper slippers
and thought how violence has no metaphorical use.
The first stop was in a transparent shower cubicle.
I began rolling my head from side to side, while I said . . .
(But you already knew her?)

"*or* to return from following after thee:"

A gentle being dropped from the sky,
in a cirrus robe embroidered with "Blame
neither past nor present." Its face was shy.
For five weeks in two cities it went by my name,
walking a bit before me, but, when I turned,
also beside me. *Now I have slain*
that impostor. In killing, I scorned
to count the cost. Since then, in each place
of sleep, a second, nude angel is found,
more vocal: Dishonour. I bent my face
towards it, to challenge; but the air between burned,

truly, with more than conventional force.
(But you already knew her?)

> "for whither thou goest, I will go;
> and where thou lodgest, I will lodge [. . .]"

I wanted to begin with a striking image,
but I'm too geometrical, I can give none,
I'm almost pure line, like a minor park sculpture
yielding up its features under too much, too long,
temperate rain – there's not a bone I could offer,
for even that would have possessed a charming whisper,
a bare suggestion of velleities, of flesh.

No Traveller Returns

A Reason to Light More Fires

Point.
It is important to win a position on the good side of the dead.
The dead are many.
Point.
The dead care only for ceremony.
They will react if you observe the forms.
Point.
Not only the proud and strifeful dead
refuse to react to human charms.
. . .
The dead are sticklers, they will understand anything
if it is manners, methodology, they will understand it as
etiquette.
Speak the word.
. . .
Betrayal belongs with the living.
It pulls up sharp,
snags, just as comb's teeth
snap unwetted hair.
The action meant to smooth through
will break the keratin flow,
fine air that should have flown like a smile,
like compromise waved through.
Death is the fall of water.
. . .
Speak the word.
Point.
After their transferral to the right hand of zero,
dignity agrees the once-differing dead.
Point.
The fear of the unquantifiable is at the root of burial.
Memorise the departed. Their days are numbered.
Point.
Epitaphs are both stark and gradual.
The event enlists us to outnumber ourselves.

No Traveller Returns

I

THE BLEEDING OBVIOUS

Two pins dancing alternately, landing in the same spot. For two pins I'd give it all up. The slash and crisscross of their silver lines, where one just has been and where the other is about to be, does not fool the eye, except in a physical reading; it is a true record of sharpness and inescapability, an impression of point zero.

Two women, their muscled arms raised and squared, their hands gripping into the other's flesh above the elbow so they are locked together, their knees too stiff and their legs too close, sway in an effortful, stylised stagger in a small space which is part of a big space, front and centre of a huge bare wooden stage. Their interlocked hand-to-arm grip, seen sideways, is almost the base line where a right angle forms at the midjoint, the vertical strained along upper arm to shoulder. Their nails are long, black, shiny, like undetailed onyx eyes. They are dressed in coarse linen like tragedy queens: one in black with black hair, one in dark purple, more like a stain than a colour, her hair entirely pasted with henna. Each looks over the other's shoulder and enunciates formally, again and again, into space:

'. . . cette nuit cruelle, Qui fut pour tout un peuple une nuit éternelle.'

'Qui te l'a dit?'

The ebony, drawn out and deeper. The vermilion, incredulous and vituperative. These remarks are not addressed by them to each other. Whoever was to receive them is long gone, but must once have been there: the sense of time past and lost presence is a function of the repeated phrases, the women's intensity. They are Andromaque and Hermione, but they no longer belong to Racine. They are strong characters, now without their men and servants.

Now, without their men and servants, they cannot do without each other. They have nothing else to say. They are compelling. We are their nation.

' . . . cette nuit cruelle, Qui fut pour tout un peuple une nuit éternelle.'

'Qui te l'a dit?'

They are locked together, their knees high and stiff, their legs like robotic pillars, staggering in a stylised, effortful pace, with no supporters, no furnishings, and no relenting. Very slowly a white canvas curtain begins to come down in front of them. It has a steel edge. This will slot in to a steel groove at the outer extreme of the stage, and click shut, irrevocably. But not yet; slowly, it is still descending. Eventually all we see is their feet, pointed and straining, in tragedians' buskins.

' . . . cette nuit cruelle, Qui fut pour tout un peuple une nuit éternelle.'

'Qui te l'a dit?'

The fearsome strength and resonance of their voices is unimpaired. Even behind the lowering curtain, the voices strike as if there were no barrier, strike direct into the ear, travelling through skull after skull to rebound as though from a total city wall. Beyond that wall there are sea cliffs. This is an island; we, the people. The spectacle is to be rejected. There is no more that can be said. If there were to be something more, it must be new.

II

ANTIGONE

It is right that this royally disobedient girl
Was a woman walled up.

It is not right
That when we recall her
The way we remember her
Is acting alone.

If,
When the dead have died,
They fall thick and fast
Into a community of likes,
And
Into a state of impermanent slumber,
No matter what was their allegiance in life,
The correct rites
Will have them clustering round your side.
They do outnumber
Any opposition.

Imagine, then,
Antigone was shut
Into the company of earth,
The squad of close-faced comrades who were there first
To applaud her
When she sought out the fraternal corpse, exposed,
With her handful of ritual burial dirt.

Be more understanding of the king her cousin's
Anger,
How it was fear.
In his conflictive city,
She mobilised the unity of ghosts.

The ability to polarise
Things that are similar –
To drive them apart –
If that proves, if that forges, regal power –

The king was right,
When he laid to rest one of her two dead brothers
With honour, and dishonoured the other.

When dust
Plus blood
Equals no more and no less
Than dust
A nation
Will stick together.

What she did reversed
What should have been
A final power.
Propitiated history trickled between her fists.
King Creon was right, to have her taken prisoner.

She had robbed him of his past in the future,
Stripped him of his future in the past,
Well finished him,
Winner of a race of one.
King without predecessors, self-perpetuating king,
        unreproducing.
A king without precedents.

Lost from his ancestors, he would live alone.
So absolute, amoral-seeming, the dead, and their code.
He shall be buried
Must join them
Will find his own self among them
The actions of his reign condemned by the order of his soul.

St. Munditia

What have you seen today, my dear?

The female tourist.

Turning to her fear, to the unlit room,
taking it in, with a kind of disregard,
opened her eyes on what lay back of the
unlined curtains, she stuck her breasts like mouths
into the dark, told them, Swallow, swallow.
So it was that sleep was wished upon her.

NEXT ON THE PROGRAMME
Is St. Munditia,
Patron Saint of Single Women,
those who live alone,
bachelor queens, spinsters, solteras.
Take a good look.
St. Munditia.
Dug up from her burial
a millenium and a third since the flesh fell off her.
She's back in church.

Was it easy for you to find, my dear?

But the preliminaries . . .

The people lounge on the london steps,
queuing for european tourist visas,
getting used to no shelter.
It can't rain all the time.
The man with the blue umbrella
stabs between the feet of fellow strangers.

Look, the would-be travellers,
they're after culture.
People hanging on to a mystique,
they hail from the wrong area.
Ticketed and quizzed
like a load of illegal orange-pickers.
Look at the faces,
those london faces,
it's everyone you don't think of,
when you think of europe's nations.
It's like going home.
"Impossible to issue."
Alien spouse.
The wife's denied.
Mother and child,
wait
wait.
Waiting to be allowed to love?
The lucky ones are stamped,
the lucky ones are charged.
What fun.
At the airport, it'll start again.
Places that don't care a straw for their prayers.
Let the journey begin.

Wasn't the weather brilliant?

Brilliant.

Magnetised by tunes, a walking jangle,
the flip of a cape, the end of the day,
jackboots under sequins, satin jockstrap,

a sunset cocktail for the happy hour,
the god apollo giving up the mike,
a new song slashed for its virus asterisk.

NEXT ON THE PROGRAMME
St. Munditia,
centuries later,
bewigged, bolted and belted with jewels,
a skimpy skeleton in a cheesecake posture,
ribs full of air,
half sitting up,
ready to launch into an aria,
glassed off like the snake room at the zoo.
Baroque.

You saw . . . ?

Spectators.

Stop.
Because there is no end to it.
She lolls,
   dolled up to look pleased by us,
pleased to be looked at in bed, by us.
Pearls are for tears. Then glass may be for pleasure:
shot hymens, lying mirrors, brandy balloons.
   What poems do not hark back to lists?
Some, ashamed of their origins, rise above
the Don Juan catalogue of love on love.
Horror on horror.
   Torn towards you,
the leaf in the heartbreak address book
yields us up. Meekly, one by one, we file
like flies over the cork stopper of a jar
whose treasured fruit glows weightless in liqueur,
packed so tight it seems to drift in shadow
cast by green glass that gives passage to light.

So, what will you do with yourself – after this?

What, forever? [laughs]

Yes.

Forever and ever? [does not laugh]

Yes!

. . .

St. Munditia,
patron saint of single women,
she whose bones are glorious in Munich,
pray for us
(and)
may she rest in peace.

Nattaraj

. . .]

dedication

[. . .

Lightning Source UK Ltd.
Milton Keynes UK
25 March 2011

169775UK00001B/66/A